RANDOM HOUSE

TREASURY *of* BEST-LOVED POEMS

3RD edition

EDITED BY LOUIS PHILLIPS
REVISED BY MELANIE FLEISHMAN

RANDOM HOUSE
REFERENCE

New York   Toronto   London   Sydney   Auckland

CONTENTS

REVISER'S PREFACE

In revising the *Random House Treasury of Best-Loved Poems*, I experienced the great pleasure of scouring shelves of libraries and bookstores, exploring literary journals, and searching the Internet to find the perfect additions.

In my search, I found that since the last revision certain poems have become beloved and some poets have gone out of favor or returned to favor. Particular poems that have become ever more important to America's written heritage include T. S. Eliot's "The Love Song of J. Alfred Prufrock," Wilfred Owen's "Dulce et Decorum Est," Emma Lazarus' "The New Colossus," e. e. cummings' "in just spring," excerpts from Edgar Lee Masters' epic *Spoon River Anthology*, William Coleridge's "The Rime of the Ancient Mariner," Emily Dickinson's "Because I could not stop for death," William Blake's "The Tyger," and Walt Whitman's "I Hear America Singing."

This edition also features the voices of increasingly popular international poets such as Rainer Maria Rilke, Charles Baudelaire, Rumi, Basho, Osip Mandlestam, Cesar Vallejo, and Joseph Brodsky. It also includes more female poets, including Sappho,

Katherine Mansfield, and Sandra Cisneros. A few contemporary poets such as Elizabeth Bishop, Charles Simic, Raymond Carver, William Stafford, John Updike, and Paul Muldoon have become necessary additions. Also featured is the prolific former Poet Laureate Billy Collins, whose poem "The Lanyard" I overheard on a National Public Radio broadcast, and which I shared with a nine-year-old aspiring poet who proudly read it aloud at school.

Many works by these poets can be found online and I encourage you to search for your favorites. What this collection offers is a careful selection of the ones that seem to yield the most joy, surprise, or satisfaction; the best-loved poems of the times.

—MELANIE FLEISHMAN

INTRODUCTION

> Come on in,
> The water's fine.
> I'll vie you
> Till I count to nine.
> If you're not
> In by then,
> Guess I'll have to
> Count to ten.

This is my invitation to all readers—"Come on in, The water's fine." Amid these pages you will encounter verses wise, verses funny, verses witty, verses sentimental, verses strange, and verses sad. You will encounter poems to move you, to amuse you— poems to add zest to the mysterious process of living.

How truly wonderful it is to hold one special verse close to your heart—to memorize the lines and recite them to yourself or to others for comfort or for pleasure. I remember quite vividly watching my own father standing up in the living room to recite Robert Service's classic ballad "The Shooting of Dan McGrew." My father would grow quite serious and then with dramatic flair the lines would flow and soar as my sisters and I listened with amazement. Why would a man who rarely read serious novels or poetry memorize so many lines? Why would he want to? I never knew the answer, but I do know that few performances entertained me quite so much.

Thus, the poems in this anthology have been collected for a wide variety of reasons. Some verses have been truly popular. Some have historical significance. Some catch a fleeting moment of American life. Some, such as "The Shooting of Dan McGrew," have personal significance for me. Some are new and should be loved. There are as many reasons for loving a particular poem as there are poems to love.

In this computer age we might find it strange to think of poems being loved at all. In an age dominated by television, motion pictures, and spreadsheets, what relevance does poetry have in our lives?

All you have to do is read some poetry to know the answer. True poets speak to us about what we feel and think and use the talents God has given them to create and re-create manifold experiences. Poetry exists in a language akin to music, in lines related to the mysterious, and somehow, in spite of everything, reminds us how important it is to speak honestly and memorably about our lives.

And so come on in. The water's fine.

—Louis Phillips

LOVE AND ROMANCE

The Passionate Shepherd to His Love

Come live with me, and be my love;
And we will all the pleasures prove
That hills and valleys, dales and fields,
Woods, or steepy mountain yields.

And we will sit upon the rocks,
Seeing the shepherds feed their flocks
By shallow rivers, to whose falls
Melodious birds sing madrigals.

And I will make thee beds of roses,
And a thousand fragrant posies;
A cap of flowers, and a kirtle
Embroidered all with leaves of myrtle;

A gown made of the finest wool
Which from our pretty lambs we pull;
Fail-lines slippers for the cold,
With buckles of the purest gold;

A belt of straw and ivy-buds,
With coral clasps and amber studs;
And if these pleasures may thee move,
Come live with me, and be my love.

The shepherd-swains shall dance and sing
For the delight each May morning;
If these delights thy mind may move,
Then love with me, and be my love.

—*Christopher Marlowe*

On Bundling

Since in bed, a maid
May bundle and be chaste.
It doth no good to burn up wood.
It is a needless waste.

—*Anonymous*

To the Virgins, to Make Much of Time

Gather ye rosebuds while ye may,
　　Old Time is still a-flying;
And this same flower that smiles to-day
　　To-morrow will be dying.

The glorious lamp of heaven, the Sun,
　　The higher he's a-getting,
The sooner will his race be run,
　　And nearer he's to setting.

That age is best which is the first,
　　When youth and blood are warmer;
But being spent, the worse, and worst
　　Times still succeed the former.

Then be not coy, but use your time;
　　And while ye may, go marry;
For having lost but once your prime,
　　You may forever tarry.

—*Robert Herrick*

To His Coy Mistress

Had we but world enough, and time,
This coyness, Lady, were no crime.
We would sit down and think which way
To walk and pass our long love's day,
Thou by the Indian Ganges' side
Shouldst rubies find; I by the tide
Of Humber would complain. I would
Love you ten years before the Flood,
And you should, if you please, refuse
Till the conversion of the Jews.
My vegetable love should grow
Vaster than empires, and more slow;
An hundred years should go to praise
Thine eyes and on thy forehead gaze'
Two hundred to adore each breast,
But thirty thousand to the rest;
An age at least to every part,
And the last age should show your heart.

For, Lady, you deserve this state,
Now would I love at lower rate.
　But at my back I always hear
Time's wingèd chariot hurrying near;
And yonder all before us lie
Deserts of vast eternity.
Thy beauty shall no more be found,
Nor, in thy marble vault, shall sound
My echoing song; then worms shall try
That long preserved virginity,
And your quaint honor turn to dust,
And into ashes all my lust:
The grave's a fine and private place,
But none, I think, do there embrace.
　Now therefore, while the youthful hue
Sits on thy skin like morning dew,
And while thy willing soul transpires
At every pore with instant fires,

Now let us sport us while we may,
And now, like amorous birds of prey,
Rather at once our time devour
Than languish in his slow-chapped power.
Let us roll all our strength and all
Our sweetness up into one ball,
And tear our pleasures with rough strife
Through the iron gates of life:
Thus, though we cannot make our sun
Stand still, yet we will make him run.

—*Andrew Marvell*

"Shall I Compare Thee"

Shall I compare thee to a summer's day?
Thou art more lovely and more temperate:
Rough winds do shake the darling buds of
    May,
And summer's lease hath all too short a date:
Sometime too hot the eye of heaven shines,
And often is his gold complexion dimmed;
And every fair from fair sometimes declines,
By chance, or nature's changing course
    untrimmed;
But thy eternal summer shall not fade,
Nor lose possession of that fair thou owest;
Not shall Death brag thou wanderest in his
    shade
When in eternal lines to time thou growest:
So long as men can breathe, or eyes can see,
So long lives this, and this gives life to thee.

—*William Shakespeare*

"My Mistress' Eyes"

My mistress' eyes are nothing like the sun;
Coral is far more red than her lips' red:
If snow be white, why then her breasts are
    dun;
If hairs be wires, black wires grow on her
    head.
I have seen roses damasked, red and white,
But no such roses see I in her cheeks;
And in some perfumes is there more delight
Than in the breath that from my mistress
    reeks.
I love to hear her speak, yet well I know
That music hath a far more pleasing sound:
I grant I never saw a goddess go,—
My mistress, when she walks, treads on the
    ground.
And yes, by heaven I think my love as rare
As any she belied with false compare.

—*William Shakespeare*

My Luve's Like a Red, Red Rose

O my Luve's like a red, red rose,
　That's newly sprung in June:
O my Luve's like the melodie
　That's sweetly played in tune!

As fair art thou, my bonnie lass,
　So deep in luve am I;
And I will luve thee still, my dear,
　Till a' the seas gang dry.

Till a' the seas gang dry, my dear,
　And the rock melt wi' the sun;
I will luve thee still, my dear,
　While the sands o' life shall run.

And fare thee weel, my only Luve,
　And fare thee weel a while!
And I will come again, my Luve,
　Though it were ten thousand mile.

—*Robert Burns*

She Walks in Beauty

She walks in beauty, like the night
   Of cloudless climes and starry skies;
And all that's best of dark and bright
   Meet in her aspect and her eyes:
Thus mellowed to that tender light
   Which heaven to gaudy day denies.

One shade the more, one ray the less,
   Had half impaired the nameless grace
Which waves in every raven tress,
   Or softly lightens o'er her face;
Where thoughts serenely sweet express
   How pure, how dear their dwelling place.

And on that cheek and o'er that brow,
   So soft, so calm, yet eloquent,
The smiles that win, the tints that glow,
   But tell of days in goodness spent,
A mind at peace with all below,
   A heart whose love is innocent!

—*George Gordon, Lord Byron*

Outwitted

He drew a circle that shut me out—
Heretic, rebel, a thing to flout.
But Love and I had the wit to win:
We drew a circle that took him in!

—*Edwin Markham*

How Do I Love Thee?

How do I love thee? Let me count the ways.
I love thee to the depth and breadth and
    height
My soul can reach, when feeling out of sight
For the Ends of Being and ideal Grace.
I love thee to the level of everyday's
Most quiet need, by sun and candle-light.
I love thee freely, as men strive for Right;
I love thee purely, as they turn from Praise.
I love thee with the passion put to use
In my old griefs, and with my childhood's
    faith.
I love thee with a love I seemed to lose
With my lost saints,—I love thee with the
    breath,
Smiles, tears, of all my life!—and, if God
    choose,
I shall but love thee better after death.

—*Elizabeth Barrett Browning*

Cuna Love Song

Many pretty flowers, red, blue,
  and yellow; we say to the girls,
"Let's go and walk among the
  flowers."
The wind comes and sways the
  flowers, the girls are like that
  when they dance; some are
  wide open, large flowers and
  some are tiny little flowers.
The birds love the sunshine and
  the starlight; the flowers smell
  sweet.
The girls are sweeter than the
  flowers.

—*Anonymous (Native American)*

Love's Philosophy

The fountains mingle with the river
 And the rivers with the Ocean;
The winds of Heaven mix for ever
 With a sweet emotion;
Nothing in the world is single;
 All things by a law divine
In one spirit meet and mingle.
 Why not I with thine?

See the mountains kiss high Heaven
 And the waves clasp one another;
No sister-flower would be forgiven
 If it disdained its brother;
And the sunlight clasps the earth
 And the moonbeams kiss the sea—
What is all this sweet work worth
 If thou kiss not me?

—*Percy Bysshe Shelley*

Patterns

I walk down the garden paths,
And all the daffodils
Are blowing, and the bright blue squills.
I walk down the patterned garden paths
In my stiff, brocaded gown.
With my powdered hair and jewelled fan,
I too am a rare
Pattern. As I wander down
The garden paths.

My dress is richly figured,
And the train
Makes a pink and silver stain
On the gravel, and the thrift
Of the borders.
Just a plate of current fashion,
Tripping by in high-heeled, ribboned shoes.
Not a softness anywhere about me,

Only whalebone and brocade.
And I sink on a seat in the shade
Of a lime tree. For my passion
Wars against the stiff brocade.
The daffodils and squills
Flutter in the breeze
As they please.
And I weep;
For the lime tree is in blossom
And one small flower has dropped upon my
    bosom.

And the plashing of waterdrops
In the marble fountain
Comes down the garden paths.
The dripping never stops.
Underneath my stiffened gown
Is the softness of a woman bathing in a
    marble basin,

A basin in the midst of hedges grown
So thick, she cannot see her lover hiding,
But she guesses he is near,
And the sliding of the water
Seems the stroking of a dear
Hand upon her.

What is Summer in a fine brocaded gown!
I should like to see it lying in a heap up on
    the ground.
All the pink and silver crumpled up on the
    ground.
I would be the pink and silver as I ran along
    the paths,
And he would stumble after,
Bewildered by my laughter.
I should see the sun flashing from his sword-
    hilt and the buckles on his shoes.
I would choose

To lead him in a maze along the patterned
    paths,
A bright and laughing maze for my heavy-
    booted lover,
Till he caught me in the shade,
And the buttons of his waistcoat bruised my
    body as he clasped me,
Aching, melting, unafraid.
With the shadows of the leaves and the
    sundrops,
And the plopping of the waterdrops,
All about us in the open afternoon—
I am very like to swoon
With the weight of this brocade,
For the sun sifts through the shade.

* * *

Underneath the fallen blossom
In my bosom,
Is a letter I have hid.
It was brought to me this morning by a rider
    from the Duke.
"Madam, we regret to inform you that Lord
    Hartwell
Died in action Thursday se'nnight."
As I read it in the white, morning sunlight,
The letters squirmed like snakes.
"Any answer, Madam" said my footman.
"No," I told him.
"See that the messenger takes some
    refreshment.
No, no answer."
And I walked into the garden,
Up and down the patterned paths,

In my stiff, correct brocade.
The blue and yellow flowers stood up
    proudly in the sun,
Each one.
I stood upright too,
Held rigid to the pattern
By the stiffness of my gown.
Up and down I walked,
Up and down.

*   *   *

In a month he would have been my husband.
In a month, here, underneath this lime,
We would have broke the pattern;
He for me, and I for him,
He is Colonel, I as Lady,
On this shady seat.

He had a whim
That sunlight carried blessing.
And I answered, "It shall be as you have
    said."
Now he is dead.

In Summer and in Winter I shall walk
Up and down
The patterned garden paths
In my stiff, brocaded gown.
The squills and daffodils
Will give place to pillared roses, and to asters,
    and to snow.
I shall go
Up and down,
In my gown.
Gorgeously arrayed,
Boned and stayed.

And the softness of my body will be guarded
    from embrace
By each button, hook, and lace.
For the man who should loose me is dead,
Fighting with the Duke of Flanders
In a pattern called a war.
Christ! What are patterns for?

—*Amy Lowell*

To My Dear and Loving Husband

If ever two were one, then surely we.
If ever man were loved by wife, then thee;
If ever wife was happy in a man,
Compare with me, ye women, if you can.
I prize thy love more than whole mines of
    gold
Or all the riches that the East doth hold.
My love is such that rivers cannot quench,
Nor ought but love from thee, give
    recompense.
Thy love is such I can no way repay,
The heavens reward thee manifold, I pray.
Then while we live, in love let's so persevere
That when we live no more, we may live
    ever.

—*Anne Bradstreet*

Ashes of Life

Love has gone and left me and the days are all
    alike;
Eat I must, and sleep I will,—and would that
    night were here!
But ah!—to lie awake and hear the slow hours
    strike!
Would that it were day again!—with twilight
    near!
Love has gone and left me and I don't know
    what to do;
This or that or what you will is all the same to
    me;
But all the things that I begin I leave before I'm
    through,—
There's little use in anything as far as I can see.
Love has gone and left me,—and the neighbors
    knock and borrow,

And life goes on forever like the gnawing of a
  mouse,—
And to-morrow and to-morrow and to-morrow
  and to-morrow
There's this little street and this little house.

—*Edna St. Vincent Millay*

Advice

Folks, I'm telling you,
Birthing is hard
And dying is mean
So get yourself
A little loving
In between.

—Langston Hughes

Remembered Music

'Tis said, the pipe and lute that charm our ears
Derive their melody from rolling spheres;
But Faith, o'erpassing speculation's bound,
Can see what sweetens every jangled sound.
We, who are parts of Adam, heard with him
The song of angels and of seraphim.
Out memory, though dull and sad, retains
Some echo still of those unearthly strains.
Oh, music is the meat of all who love,
Music uplifts the soul to realms above.
The ashes glow, the latent fires increase:
We listen and are fed with joy and peace.

—*Rumi*

The Beauty of the Heart

The beauty of the heart
is the lasting beauty:
its lips give to drink
of the water of life.
Truly it is the water,
that which pours,
and the one who drinks.
All three become one when
your talisman is shattered.
That oneness you can't know
by reasoning.

—*Rumi*

The Night Has a Thousand Eyes

The Night has a thousand eyes,
    And the day but one;
Yet the light of the bright world dies
    With the dying sun.
The mind has a thousand eyes,
    And the heart but one:
Yet the light of a whole life dies
    When love is done.

—*Francis William Bourdillon*

Camomile Tea

Outside the sky is light with stars;
There's a hollow roaring from the sea.
And, alas! for the little almond flowers,
The wind is shaking the almond tree.

How little I thought, a year ago,
In the horrible cottage upon the Lee
That he and I should be sitting so
And sipping a cup of camomile tea.

Light as feathers the witches fly,
The horn of the moon is plain to see;
By a firefly under a jonquil flower
A goblin toasts a bumble-bee.

We might be fifty, we might be five,
So snug, so compact, so wise are we!
Under the kitchen-table leg
My knee is pressing against his knee.

Our shutters are shut, the fire is low,
The tap is dripping peacefully;
The saucepan shadows on the wall
Are black and round and plain to see.

—*Katherine Mansfield*

Be Kind to Me

Gongyla; I ask only
that you wear the cream
white dress when you come
Desire darts about your
loveliness, drawn down in
circling flight at sight of it
and I am glad, although
once I too quarrelled
with Aphrodite
to whom
I pray that you will
come soon

—*Sappho*

Without Warning

Without warning
as a whirlwind
swoops on an oak
Love shakes my heart

—*Sappho*

Even When She Walks...

Even when she walks she seems to dance!
Her garments writhe and glisten like long
   snakes
obedient to the rhythm of the wands
by which a fakir wakens them to grace.

Like both the desert and the desert sky
insensible to human suffering,
and like the ocean's endless labyrinth
she shows her body with indifference.

Precious minerals are her polished eyes,
and in her strange symbolic nature
angel and sphinx unite,
where diamonds, gold, and steel dissolve into
   one light,
shining forever, useless as a star,
the sterile woman's icy majesty.

—Charles Baudelaire

To Celia

Drink to me only with thine eyes,
And I will pledge with mine;
Or leave a kiss but in the cup
And I'll not look for wine.
The thirst that from the soul doth rise
Doth ask a drink divine;
But might I of Jove's nectar sup,
I would not change for thine.

I sent thee late a rosy wreath,
Not so much honoring thee
As giving it a hope that there
It could not wither'd be;
But thou thereon didst only
    breathe
And sent'st it back to me;
Since when it grows,
and smells, I swear,
Not of itself, but thee!

—*Ben Jonson*

The Baite

Come live with mee, and bee my love.
And we will some new pleasures prove
Of golden sands, and christall brookes,
With silken lines, and silver hookes.

There will the river whispering runne
Warm'd by thy eyes, more than the Sunne.
And there th' inamor'd fish will stay,
Begging themselves they may betray.

When thou wilt swimme in that live bath,
Each fish, which every channel hath,
Will amorously to thee swimme,
Gladder to catch thee, then thou him.

If thou, to be so seene, beest loathe,
By Sunne, or Moone, thou darkest both,
And if my selfe have leave to see,
I need not their light, having thee.

Let others freeze with angling reeds,
And cut their legges, with shells and weeds,
Or treacherously poore fish beset,
With strangling snare, or windowie net:

Let coarse bold hands, from slimy nest
The bedded fish in banks out-wrest,
Or curious traitors, sleavesilke flies
Bewitch poore fishes wandering eyes.

For thee, thou needst no such deceit,
For thou thy selfe art thine owne bait;
That fish that is not catch'd nearby,
Alas, is wiser farre then I.

—*John Donne*

Ask Me

Some time when the river is ice ask me
mistakes I have made. Ask me whether
what I have done is my life. Others
have come in their slow way into
my thought, and some have tried to help
or to hurt: ask me what difference
their strongest love or hate has made.
I will listen to what you say.
You and I can turn and look
at the silent river and wait. We know
the current is there, hidden; and there
are comings and goings from miles away
that hold the stillness exactly before us.
What the river says, that is what I say.

—*William Stafford*

Waiting

Left off the highway and
down the hill. At the
bottom, hang another left.
Keep bearing left. The road
will make a Y. Left again.
There's a creek on the left.
Keep going. Just before
the road ends, there'll be
another road. Take it
and no other. Otherwise,
your life will be ruined
forever. There's a log house
with a shake roof, on the left.
It's not that house. It's
the next house, just over

a rise. The house
where trees are laden with
fruit. Where phlox, forsythia,
and marigold grow. It's
the house where the woman
stands in the doorway
wearing the sun in her hair. The one
who's been waiting
all this time.
The woman who loves you.
The one who can say,
"What's kept you?"

—*Raymond Carver*

NATURE AND THE
PASSING OF TIME

Nature

a fond mother, when the day is o'er,
Leads by the hand her little child to bed,
Half willing, half reluctant to be led,
And leave his broken playthings on the floor,
Still gazing at them through the open door,
Nor wholly reassured and comforted
By promises of others in their stead,
Which, though more splendid, may not please
   him more;
So Nature deals with us, and takes away
Our playthings one by one, and by the hand
Leads us to rest so gently, that we go
Scarce knowing if we wish to go or stay,
Being too full of sleep to understand
How far the unknown transcends the what we
   know.

—*Henry Wadsworth Longfellow*

I Wandered Lonely as a Cloud

I wandered lonely as a cloud
That floats on high o'er vales and hills,
When all at once I saw a crowd,
A host, of golden daffodils,
Beside the lake, beneath the trees
Fluttering and dancing in the breeze.

Continuous as the stars that shine
And twinkle on the Milky Way,
They stretched in never-ending line
Along the margin of a bay.
Ten thousand saw I at a glance,
Tossing their heads in sprightly dance.

The waves beside them danced; but they
Outdid the sparkling waves in glee;
A poet could not but be gay,
In such a jocund company;

I gazed—and gazed—but little thought
What wealth the show to me had brought:
For oft, when on my couch I lie
In vacant or in pensive mood,
They flash upon that inward eye
Which is the bliss of solitude;
And then my heart with pleasure fills,
And dances with the daffodils.

—*William Wordsworth*

The Year's at the Spring

The year's at the spring
And the day's at the morn;
Morning's at seven;
The hillside's dew-pearled;
The lark's on the wing;
The snail's on the thorn:
God's in his heaven
All's right with the world!

—*Robert Browning*

Spring

When daffodils begin to peer,
   With heigh! the doxy, over the dale,
Why, then comes in the sweet o' the year;
   For the red blood reigns in the winter's
     pale.

The white sheet bleaching on the hedge,
   With heigh! the sweet birds, O, how they
     sing!
Doth set my pugging tooth on edge,
   For a quart of ale is a dish for a king.

The lark, that tirra-lirra chants,
   With heigh! with heigh! the thrush and they
     jay,
Are summer songs for me and my aunts,
   While we lie tumbling in the hay.

—*William Shakespeare*

Loveliest of Trees

Loveliest of tress, the cherry now
Is hung with bloom along the bough,
And stands about the woodland ride
Wearing white for Eastertide.

Now, of my threescore years and then,
Twenty will not come again,
And take from seventy springs a score,
It only leaves me fifty more.

And since to look at things in bloom
Fifty springs are little room,
About the woodlands I will go
To see the cherry hung with snow.

—*A. E. Housman*

'Tis the Last Rose of Summer

'Tis the last rose of Summer,
  Left blooming alone;
All her lovely companions
  Are faded and gone;
No flower of her kindred,
  No rosebud is nigh,
To reflect back her blushes,
  Or give sigh for sigh!

I'll not leave thee, thou lone one,
  To pine on the stem;
Since the lovely are sleeping,
  Go sleep thou with them.
Thus kindly I scatter
  Thy leaves o'er the bed
Where thy mates of the garden
  Lie scentless and dead.

So soon my I follow,
    When friendships decay,
And from Love's shining circle
    The gems drop away!
When true hearts lie withered,
    And fond ones are flown,
Oh! who would inhabit
    This bleak world alone?

—*Thomas Moore*

Spring and Fall:
To a Young Child

Márgarét, are you gríeving
Over Goldengrove unleaving?
Léaves, líke the things of man, you
With your fresh thoughts care for, can you?
Áh! ás the heart grows older
It will come to such sights colder
By and by, nor spare a sigh
Though worlds of wanwood leafmeal lie;
And yet you wíll weep and know why.
Now no matter, child, the name:
Sórrow's spríngs áre the same.
Nor mouth had, no nor mind, expressed
What heart heard of, ghost guessed:
It ís the blight man was born for,
It ís Margaret you mourn for.

—*Gerard Manley Hopkins*

The Darkling Thrush

I leant upon a coppice gate
  When Frost was spectre-grey,
And Winter's dregs made desolate
  The weakening eye of day.
The tangled bine-stems scored the sky
  Like strings from broken lyres,
And all mankind that haunted nigh
  Had sought their household fires.

The land's sharp features seemed to be
  The Century's corpse outleant
His crypt the cloudy canopy,
  The wind his death-lament.
The ancient pulse of germ and birth
  Was shrunken hard and dry,
And every spirit upon earth
  Seemed fervourless as I.

At once a voice arose among
  The bleak twigs overhead
In a full-hearted evensong
  Of joy illimited;
An agèd thrush, frail, gaunt, and small,
  In blast-beruffled plume,
Had chosen thus to fling his soul
  Upon the growing gloom.

So little cause for carolings
  Of such ecstatic sound
Was written on terrestrial things
  Afar or nigh around,
That I could think there trembled through
  His happy good-night air
Some blessed Hope, whereof he knew
  And I was unaware.

—*Thomas Hardy*

Fall, Leaves, Fall

Fall, leaves, fall; die, flowers, away;
Lengthen night and shorten day;
Every leaf speaks bliss to me,
Fluttering from the autumn tree.
I shall smile when wreaths of snow
Blossom where the rose should grow;
I shall sing when night's decay
Ushers in a drearier day.

—*Emily Brontë*

Stopping by Woods
on a Snowy Evening

Whose woods there are I think I know.
His house is in the village though;
He will not see me stopping here
To watch his woods fill up with snow.

My little horse must think it queer
To stop without a farmhouse near
Between the woods and frozen lake
The darkest evening of the year.

He gives his harness bells a shake
To ask if there is some mistake.
The only other sound's the sweep
Of easy wind and downy flake.

The woods are lovely, dark and deep.
But I have promises to keep,
And miles to go before I sleep,
And miles to go before I sleep.

—*Robert Frost*

The Ages of Man

At ten, a child; at twenty, wild;
　At thirty, tame if ever;
At forty, wise; at fifty, rich;
　At sixty, good or never.

—*Anonymous*

The Snowstorm

Announced by all the trumpets of the sky,
Arrives the snow, and, driving o'er the fields,
Seems nowhere to alight: the whited air
Hides hills and woods, the river, and the
    heaven
And veils the farmhouse at the garden's end.
The sled and traveler stopped, the courier's
    feet
Delayed, all friends shut out, the housemates
    sit
Around the radiant fireplace, enclosed
In a tumultuous privacy of storm.

  Come see the north wind's, masonry.
Out of an unseen quarry evermore
Furnished with tile, the fierce artificer
Curves his white bastions with projected roof
Round every windward stake, or tree, or door.

Speeding, the myriad-handed, his wild work
So fanciful, so savage, nought cares he
For number or proportion. Mockingly,
On coop or kennel he hangs Parian wreaths;
A swan-like form invests the hidden thorn;
Fills up the farmer's lane from wall to wall,
Maugre the farmer's sighs; and, at the gate,
A tapering turret overtops the work.
And when his hours are numbered, and the
    world
Is all his own, retiring, as he were not,
Leaves, when the sun appears, astonished Art
To mimic in slow structures, stone by stone,
Built in an age, the mad wind's night-work,
The frolic architecture of the snow.

—*Ralph Waldo Emerson*

Snowflakes

Out of the bosom of the air,
   Out of the cloud-folds of her garments
     shaken,
Over the woodlands brown and bare,
   Over the harvest-fields forsaken,
    Silent, and soft, and slow
    Descends the snow.

Even as our cloudy fancies take
   Suddenly shape in some divine expression,
Even as the troubled heart doth make
In the white countenance confession,
   The troubled sky reveals
   The grief it feels.

This is the poem of the air,
　　Slowly in silent syllables recorded;
This is the secret of despair,
　　Long in its cloudy bosom hoarded,
　　　How whispered and revealed
　　　To wood and field.

—*John Greenleaf Whittier*

Fog

The fog comes on little cat feet.
It sits looking over harbor and city,
On silent haunches and then moves on.

—*Carl Sandburg*

On Aging

When you see me sitting quietly,
Like a sack left on the shelf,
Don't think I need your chattering.
I'm listening to myself.
Hold! Stop! Don't pity me!
Hold! Stop your sympathy!
Understanding if you got it,
Otherwise I'll do without it!

When my bones are stiff and aching
And my feet won't climb the stair,
I will only ask one favor:
Don't bring me no rocking chair.

When you see me walking, stumbling,
Don't study and get it wrong.
'Cause tired don't mean lazy
And every goodbye ain't gone.

I'm the same person I was back then,
A little less hair, a little less chin,
A lot less lungs and much less wind.
But ain't I lucky I can still breathe in.

—*Maya Angelou*

Ode to a Nightingale

My heart aches, and a drowsy numbness
        pains
    My sense, as though of hemlock I had
        drunk,
Or emptied some dull opiate to the drains
    One minute past, and Lethe-wards had
        Sunk:
'Tis not through envy of thy happy lot,
    But being too happy in thine happiness,—
        That thou, light-wingèd Dryad of the
            trees,
            In some melodious plot
    Of beechen green, and shadows
        numberless,
        Singest of summer in full-throated ease.

O for a draught of vintage! that hath been
    Cool'd a long age in the deep-delvèd earth,

Tasting of Flora and the country–green,
  Dance, and Provençal song, and sunburnt
    mirth!
O for a beaker full of the warm South,
  Full of the true, the blushful Hippocrene,
    With beaded bubbles winking at the brim,
      And purple-stainèd mouth;
That I might drink, and leave the world
    unseen,
And with thee fade away into the forest
    dim:

Fade far away, dissolve, and quite forget
  What thou among the leaves hast never
    known,
The weariness, the fever, and the fret
  Here, where men sit and ear each other
    groan;

Where palsy shakes a few, sad, last gray hairs,
  Where youth grows pale, and spectre-thin,
    and dies;
Where but to think is to be full of sorrow
    And leaden-eyed despairs,
  Where Beauty cannot keep her lustrous
    eyes,
  Or new Love pine at them beyond to-morrow.

Away! away! for I will fly to thee,
  Not charioted by Bacchus and his pards,
But on the viewless wings of Poesy,
  Though the dull brain perplexes and
    retards:
Already with thee! tender is the night,
  And haply the Queen Moon is on her
    throne,
  Clustered around by all her starry Fays;

But here there is no light,
Save what from heaven is with the breezes
    blown
Through verdurous glooms and winding
    mossy ways.

I cannot see what flowers are at my feet,
    Nor what soft incense hangs upon the
        boughs,
    But, in embalmèd darkness, guess each sweet
    Wherewith the seasonable month endows
    The grass, the thicket, and the fruit-tree wild;
    White hawthorn, and the pastoral
        eglantine;
        Fast fading violets covered up in leaves:
            And mid-May's eldest child,
    The coming musk-rose, full of dewy wine,
        The murmurous haunt of flies on summer
            eves.

Darkling I listen; and, for many a time
  I have been half in love with easeful Death,
Call'd him soft names in many a musèd rhyme,
  To take into the air my quiet breath;
Now more than ever seems it rich to die,
  To cease upon the midnight with no pain,
    While thou art pouring forth thy soul
     abroad
      In such an ecstasy!
  Still wouldst thou sing, and I have ears in
     vain—
    To thy high requiem become a sod.

Thou wast not born for death, immortal Bird!
  No hungry generations tread thee down;
The voice I hear this passing night was heard
  In ancient days by emperor and clown:
Perhaps the self-same song that found a path
  Through the sad heart of Ruth, when, sick
    for home,

She stood in tears amid the alien corn;
   The same that oft-times hath
Charmed magic casements, opening on the
      foam
   Of perilous seas, in faery lands forlorn.

Forlorn! the very word is like a bell
   To toll me back from thee to my sole self!
Adieu! the fancy cannot cheat so well
   As she is famed to do, deceiving elf.
Adieu! adieu! thy plaintive anthem fades
   Past the near meadows, over the still
         stream,
      Up the hill-side; and now 'tis buried
      deep
      In the next valley-glades:
   Was it a vision, or a walking dream?
      Fled is that music:—do I wake or sleep?

—*John Keats*

Miniver Cheevy

Miniver Cheevy, child of scorn,
   Grew lean while he assailed the seasons;
He wept that he was ever born.
   And he had reasons.

Miniver loved the days of old
   When swords were bright and steeds were
     prancing;
The vision of a warrior bold
   Would set him dancing.

Miniver sighed for what was not,
   And dreamed, and rested from his labours;
He dreamed of Thebes and Camelot,
   And Priam's neighbours.

Miniver mourned the ripe renown
   That made so many a name so fragrant;
He mourned Romance, now on the town;
   And Art, a vagrant.

Miniver loved the Medici,
  Albeit he had never seen one;
He would have sinned incessantly
  Could he have been one.

Miniver cursed the commonplace
  And eyed a khaki suit with loathing;
He missed the medieval grace
  Of iron clothing.

Miniver scorned the gold he sought;
  But sore annoyed was he without it;
Miniver thought, and thought, and thought,
  And thought about it.

Miniver Cheevy, born too late,
  Scratched his head and kept on thinking;
Miniver coughed, and called it fate,
  And kept on drinking.

—*Edwin Arlington Robinson*

Richard Cory

Whenever Richard Cory went downtown,
　We people on the pavement looked at him:
He was a gentleman from sole to crown,
　Clean favored, and imperially slim.

And he was always quietly arrayed,
　And he was always human when he talked;
But still he fluttered pulses when he said,
　"Good morning," and he glittered when he
　　walked.

And he was rich—yes, richer than a king,
　And admirably schooled in every grace:
In fine, we thought that he was everything
　To make us wish that we were in his place.
So on we worked, and waited for the light,
　And went without the meat, and cursed the
　　bread;

And Richard Cory, one calm summer night,
  Went home and put a bullet through his
    head.

—*Edwin Arlington Robinson*

The Raven

Once upon a midnight dreary, while I
 pondered, weak and weary,
Over many a quaint and curious volume of
 forgotten lore—
While I nodded nearly napping, suddenly
 there came a tapping,
As of someone gently rapping, rapping at my
 chamber door.

" 'Tis some visitor," I muttered, "tapping at
 my chamber door—
 Only this and nothing more."

Ah, distinctly I remember it was in the bleak
 December;
And each separate dying ember wrought its
 ghost upon the floor.

Eagerly I wished the morrow;—vainly I had
     sought to borrow
From my books surcease of sorrow—sorrow
     for the lost Lenore—
For the rare and radiant maiden whom
     angels name Lenore—
          Nameless here for evermore.

And the silken, sad, uncertain rustling of each
     purple curtain
Thrilled me—filled me with fantastic terrors
     never felt before;
So that now, to still the beating of my heart, I
     stood repeating
"'Tis some visitor entreating entrance at my
chamber door—
Some late visitor entreating entrance at my
     chamber door—
          This it is and nothing more."

Presently my soul grew stronger; hesitating
    then no longer,
"Sir," said I, "or Madam, truly your
    forgiveness I implore;
But the fact is I was napping, and so gently
    you came rapping,
And so faintly you came tapping, tapping at
    my chamber door,
That I scarce was sure I heard you"—here I
  opened wide the door;
        Darkness there and nothing more.

Deep into that darkness peering, long I stood
  there wondering, fearing,
Doubting, dreaming dreams no mortal ever
  dared to dream before;
But the silence was unbroken, and the
  stillness gave no token,

And the only word there spoken was the
   whispered word, "Lenore!"
This I whispered, and an echo murmured
   back the word "Lenore!"
      Merely this and nothing more.

Back into the chamber turning, all my soul
   within me burning,
Soon again I heard a tapping somewhat
   louder than before.
"Surely," said I, "surely that is something at
   my window lattice;
Let me see, then, what thereat is, and this
   mystery explore—
Let my heart be still a moment and this
   mystery explore—
      'Tis the wind and nothing more!"

Open here I flung the shutter, when, with
  many a flirt and flutter
In there stepped a stately Raven of the saintly
  days of yore.
Not the least obeisance made he; not a
  minute stopped or stayed he;
But, with mien of lord or lady, perched above
  my chamber door—
Perched upon a bust of Pallas just above my
  chamber door—
    Perched, and sat, and nothing more

Then this ebony bird beguiling my sad fancy
  into smiling,
By the grave and stern decorum of the
    countenance it wore,
"Though thy crest be shorn and shaven,
    thou," I said, "art sure no craven,

Ghastly grim and ancient Raven wandering
    from the Nightly shore—
Tell me what thy lordly name is on the
    Night's Plutonian shore!"
      Quoth the Raven, "Nevermore."

Much I marveled this ungainly fowl to hear
    discourse so plainly,
Though its answer little meaning, little
    relevancy, bore;
For we cannot help agreeing that no living
    human being
Ever yet was blessed with seeing bird above
    his chamber door—
Bird or beast upon the sculptured bust above
    his chamber door,
      With such name as "Nevermore."

But the Raven, sitting lonely on the placid
    bust, spoke only
That one word, as if his soul in that one word
    he did outpour.
Nothing farther then he uttered—not a
    feather then he fluttered—
Till I scarcely more than muttered, "Other
    friends have flown before—
On the morrow he will leave me, as my hopes
    have flown before.
        Then the bird said, "Nevermore."

Startled at the stillness broken by reply so
    aptly spoken,
"Doubtless," said I, "what it utters is its only
    stock and store,
Caught from some unhappy master whom
    unmerciful Disaster

Followed fast and followed faster till his
    songs one burden bore—
Till the dirges of his hope that melancholy
    burden bore
      Of "Never—nevermore."

But the Raven still beguiling all my fancy
    into smiling,
Straight I wheeled a cushioned seat in front
    of bird, and bust and door;
Then, upon the velvet sinking, I betook
    myself to linking
Fancy unto fancy, thinking what this ominous
    bird of yore—
What his grim, ungainly, ghastly, gaunt, and
    ominous bird of yore
      Meant in croaking "Nevermore!"

This I sat engaged in guessing, but no
     syllable expressing
To the fowl whose fiery eyes now burned into
     my bosom's core;
This and more I sat divining,
     with my head at ease reclining
On the cushion's velvet lining that the
     lamplight gloated o'er,
But whose velvet violet lining, with the
     lamplight gloating o'er,
          She shall press, ah! nevermore!

Then methought the air grew denser,
     perfumed form an unseen censer
Swung by seraphim, whose footfalls tinkled
     on the tufted floor.
"Wretch," I cried, "thy God hath lent thee,—
     by these angels he hath sent thee
Respite,—respite and nepenthe from the
     memories of Lenore!

Quaff, O, quaff this kind nepenthe, and forget
    this lost Lenore!"
    Quoth the Raven, "Nevermore!"

"Prophet!" said I, "thing of evil!—prophet
    still, if bird or devil!
Whether tempter sent, or whether tempest
    tossed thee here ashore,
Desolate yet all undaunted, on this desert
    land enchanted,—
On this home by Horror haunted,—tell me
    truly, I implore,—
Is there—is there balm in Gilead?—tell me,
    tell me, I implore!"
    Quoth the Raven, "Nevermore!"

"Prophet!" said I, "thing of evil!—prophet
    still, if bird or devil!
By that heaven that bends above us—by that
    God we both adore,
Tell this soul with sorrow laden, if, within the
    distant Aidenn,
It shall clasp a sainted maiden, whom the
    angels name Lenore,
Clasp a fair and radiant maiden, whom the
    angels name Lenore!"
      Quoth the Raven, "Nevermore!"

"Be that word our sign of parting, bird or
    fiend!" I shrieked, upstarting,—
"Get thee back into the tempest and the
    night's Plutonian shore!
Leave no black plume as a token of that lie
    thy soul hath spoken!

Leave my loneliness unbroken!—quit the
     bust above my door!
Take thy beak from out my heart, and take thy
     form from off my door!"
          Quoth the Raven, "Nevermore!"

And the Raven, never flitting, still is sitting,
     still is sitting
On the pallid bust of Pallas, just above my
     chamber door;
And his eyes have all the seeming of a
     demon's that is dreaming,
And the lamp-light o'er him streaming throws
     his shadow on the floor;
And my soul from out that shadow that lies
     floating on the floor
          Shall be lifted—nevermore!

—*Edgar Allan Poe*

A Bird Came Down the Walk

A Bird came down the Walk—
He did not know I saw—
He bit an Angleworm in halves
And ate the fellow, raw,

And then he rank a Dew
From a convenient Grass—
And then hopped sidewise to the Wall
To let a Beetle pass—

He glanced with rapid eyes
That hurried all around—
They looked like frightened Beads,
    I thought—
He stirred his Velvet Head

Like one in danger, Cautious,
I offered him a Crumb
And he unrolled his feathers
And rowed him softer home—

Than Oars divide the Ocean,
Too silver for a seam—
Or Butterflies, off Banks of Noon
Leap, plashless as they swim.

—*Emily Dickinson*

My Heart's in the Highlands

Farewell to the Highlands, farewell to the
    North,
The birth-place of valor, the country of worth!
Wherever I wander, wherever I rove,
The hills of the Highlands for ever I love.

  My heart's in the Highlands, my heart is
    not here,
  My heart's in the Highlands a-chasing the
    deer,
  A-chasing the wild deer and following the
    roe—
  My heart's in the Highlands, wherever I go.

Farewell to the mountains high-covered with
    snow,
Farewell to the straths and green valleys
    below,

Farewell to the forests and wild-hanging
   woods,
Farewell to the torrents and loud-pouring
   floods!

  My heart's in the Highlands, my heart is
     not here,
  My heart's in the Highlands a-chasing the
     deer,
  A-chasing the wild deer and following the
     roe—
  My heart's in the Highlands, wherever I
     go!

—*Robert Burns*

Woodchucking

I have chased fugacious woodchucks over
   many leagues of land,
But at last they've always vanished in a round
   hole in the sand;
And though I've been woodchucking many
   times—upon my soul—
I have never bagged my woodchuck, for he
   always found his hole.

I have chased my hot ambitions through the
   meadow white with flowers,
Chased them through the clover blossoms,
   chased them through the orchard
   bowers;
Chased them through the old scrub pastures
   till with weariness of soul
I at last have seen them vanish like a
   woodchuck in his hole.

But there's fun in chasing woodchucks, and
    I'll chase the vision still,
If it leads me through the dark pine woods
    and up the stony hill
There's a glorious expectation that still
    lingers in my soul,
That some day I'll catch that woodchuck ere
    he slides into his hole.

—*Anonymous*

in Just-spring

in Just-
spring   when the world is mud-
luscious the little lame baloonman

whistles   far   and wee

and eddyandbill come
running from marbles and
piracies and it's
spring

when the world is puddle-wonderful

the queer
old baloonman whistles
far   and   wee
and bettyandisbel come dancing

from hop-scotch and jump-rope and

it's
spring
and
   the
   goat-footed

baloonman   whistles
far
and
wee

—*e. e. cummings*

The Tyger

Tyger! Tyger! burning bright
In the forests of the night,
What immortal hand or eye
Could frame thy fearful symmetry?

In what distant deeps or skies
Burnt the fire of thine eyes?
On what wings dare he aspire?
What the hand, dare seize the fire?

And what shoulder, & what art,
Could twist the sinews of thy heart?
And when thy heart began to beat,
What dread hand? & what dread feet?

What the hammer? what the chain?
In what furnace was thy brain?
What the anvil? what dread grasp
Dare its deadly terrors clasp?

When the stars threw down their spears,
And water'd heaven with their tears,
Did he smile his work to see?
Did he who made the Lamb make thee?

Tyger! Tyger! burning bright
In the forests of the night,
What immortal hand or eye
Dare frame thy fearful symmetry?

—*William Blake*

The Panther In the Jardin des Plantes, Paris

His vision, from the constantly passing bars,
has grown so weary that it cannot hold
anything else. It seems to him there are
a thousand bars; and behind the bars, no world.
As he paces in cramped circles, over and over,
the movement of his powerful soft strides
is like a ritual dance around a center
in which a mighty will stands paralyzed.
Only at times, the curtain of the pupils
lifts, quietly—. An image enters in,
rushes down through the tensed, arrested
     muscles,
plunges into the heart and is gone.

—*Rainer Maria Rilke*

It Is Not Growing Like a Tree'

It is not growing like a tree
In bulk, doth make Man better be;
Or standing long an oak, three hundred year.
To fall a log at last, dry, bald, and sere:
     A lily of a day
     Is fairer far in May,
  Although it fall and die that night:
  It was the plant and flower of Light.
In small proportions we just beauties see;
And in short measures life may perfect be—.

—*Ben Jonson*

The Redwoods

Mountains are moving, rivers
are hurrying. But we
are still.

We have the thoughts of giants—
clouds, and at night the stars.

And we have names—guttural, grotesque—
Hamet, Og—names with no syllables.

And perish, one by one, our roots
gnawed by the mice. And fall.

And are too slow for death, and change
to stone. Or else too quick,

like candles in a fire. Giants
are lonely. We have waited long

for someone. By our waiting, surely
there must be someone at whose touch

our boughs would bend; and hands
to gather us; a spirit

to whom we are light as the hawthorn tree.
O if there is a poet.

let him come now! We stand at the Pacific
like great unmarried girls,

turning in our heads the stars and clouds,
considering whom to please.

—*Louis Simpson*

The Old Pond

An old silent pond…
A frog jumps into the pond,
Splash! Silence again.

—Basho

Behind Stowe

I heard an elf go whistling by,
A whistle sleek as moonlit grass,
That drew me like a silver string
To where the dusty, pale moths fly,
And make a magic as they pass;
And there I heard a cricket sing.

His singing echoed through and through
The dark under a windy tree
Where glinted little insects' wings.
His singing split the sky in two.
The halves fell either side of me,
And I stood straight, bright with moon-wings.

—*Elizabeth Bishop*

Because I could not
stop for Death—

Because I could not stop for Death—
He kindly stopped for me—
The Carriage held but just Ourselves—
And Immortality.

We slowly drove—He knew no haste
And I had put away
My labor and my leisure too,
For His Civility—

We passed the School, where Children strove
At Recess—in the Ring—
We passed the Fields of Gazing Grain—
We passed the Setting Sun—

Or rather—He passed us—
The Dews drew quivering and chill—
For only Gossamer, my Gown—
My Tippet—only Tulle—

We paused before a House that seemed
A Swelling of the Ground—
The Roof was scarcely visible—
The Cornice—in the Ground—

Since then—'tis Centuries—and yet
Feels shorter than the Day
I first surmised the Horses' Heads
Were toward Eternity—

—*Emily Dickinson*

Love Song of
J. Alfred Prufrock

`io credesse che mia risposta fosse
A persona che mai tornasse al mondo,
Questa fiamma staria senza piu scosse.
Ma perciocche giammai di questo fondo
Non torno vivo alcun, s'i'odo il vero,
Senza tema d'infamia ti rispondo.

Let us go then, you and I,
When the evening is spread out against the sky
Like a patient etherized upon a table;
Let us go, through certain half-deserted streets,
The muttering retreats
Of restless nights in one-night cheap hotels
And sawdust resturants with oyster-shells
Streets that follow like a tedious argument
Of insidious intent

To lead you to an overwhelming question...
Oh, do not ask, "What is it? "
Let us go and make our visit.
In the room the women come and go
Talking of Michelangelo.

The yellow fog that rubs its back upon the
    window-panes
The yellow smoke that rubs its muzzle on the
    window-panes
Licked its tongue into the corners of the
    evening.
Lingered upon the pools that stand in drains.
Let fall upon its back the soot that falls from
    chimneys.
Slipped by the terrace, made a sudden leap,
And seeing that it was a soft October night,
Curled once about the house, and fell asleep.

And indeed there will be time
For the yellow smoke that slides along the
    street,
Rubbing its back upon the window-panes;
There will be time, there will be time
To prepare a face to meet the faces that you
    meet;
There will be time to murder and create,
And time for all the works and days of hands
That lift and drop a question on your plate;
Time for you and time for me.
And time yet for a hundred indecisions,
And for a hundred visions and revisions,
Before the taking of a toast and tea.

In the room the women come and go
Talking of Michelangelo.

And indeed there will be time
To wonder, "Do I dare?" and, "Do I dare?"
Time to turn back and descend the stair,
With a bald spot in the middle of my hair—
[They will say: "How his hair is growing
    thin!"]
My morning coat, my collar mounting firmly
    to the chin,
My necktie rich and modest, but asserted by a
    simple pin—
[They will say: "But how his arms and legs are
    thin!"]
Do I dare
Disturb the universe?
In a minute there is time
For decisions and revisions which a minute will
    reverse.
For I have known them all already, known them
    all:

Have known the evenings, mornings,
    afternoons,
I have measured out my life with coffee spoons;
I know the voices dying with a dying fall
Beneath the music from a farther room.
So how should I presume?

And I have known the eyes already, known
    them all—
The eyes that fix you in a formulated phrase,
And when I am formulated, sprawling on a pin,
When I am pinned and wriggling on the wall,
Then how should I begin
To spit out all the butt-ends of my days and
    ways?
And how should I presume?
And I have known the arms already, known
    them all—

Arms that are braceleted and white and bare
[But in the lamplight, downed with light
  brown hair!]
Is it perfume from a dress
That makes me so digress?
Arms that lie along a table, or wrap about a
  shawl.
And should I then presume?
And how should I begin?

                  *   *   *

Shall I say, I have gone at dusk through narrow
  streets
And watched the smoke that rises from the pipes
Of lonely men in shirt-sleeves, leaning out of
  windows? . . .
I should have been a pair of ragged claws
Scuttling across the floors of silent seas.

* * *

And the afternoon, the evening, sleeps so
    peacefully!
Smoothed by long fingers,
Asleep. . . tired . . . or it malingers,
Stretched on the floor, here beside you and me.
Should I, after tea and cakes and ices,
Have the strength to force the moment to its
    crisis?
But though I have wept and fasted, wept and
    prayed,
Though I have seen my head [grown slightly
    bald] brought in upon a platter,
I am no prophet—and here's no great matter;
I have seen the moment of my greatness flicker,
And I have seen the eternal Footman hold my
    coat, and snicker,
And in short, I was afraid.

And would it have been worth it, after all,
After the cups, the marmalade, the tea,
Among the porcelain, among some talk of you
    and me,
Would it have been worth while,
To have bitten off the matter with a smile,
To have squeezed the universe into a ball
To roll it toward some overwhelming question,
To say: "I am Lazarus, come from the dead,
Come back to tell you all, I shall tell you all"—
If one, settling a pillow by her head,
  Should say: "That is not what I meant at all.
  That is not it, at all."

And would it have been worth it, after all,
Would it have been worth while,
After the sunsets and the dooryards and the
    sprinkled streets,

After the novels, after the teacups, after the
    skirts that trail along the floor—
And this, and so much more?—
It is impossible to say just what I mean!
But as if a magic lantern threw the nerves in
    patterns on a screen:
Would it have been worth while
If one, settling a pillow, or throwing off a
    shawl,
And turning toward the window, should say:
    "That is not it at all,
    That is not what I meant, at all."

*   *   *

No! I am not Prince Hamlet, nor was meant to
    be;
Am an attendant lord, one that will do
To swell a progress, start a scene or two,
Advise the prince; no doubt, an easy tool,

Deferential, glad to be of use,
Politic, cautious, and meticulous;
Full of high sentence, but a bit obtuse;
At times, indeed, almost ridiculous—
Almost, at times, the Fool.

I grow old . . . I grow old . . .
I shall wear the bottoms of my trousers rolled.

Shall I part my hair behind? Do I dare to eat a
  peach?
I shall wear white flannel trousers, and walk
  upon the beach.
I have heard the mermaids singing, each to
  each.

I do not think that they will sing to me.

I have seen them riding seaward on the waves
Combing the white hair of the waves blown
    back
When the wind blows the water white and
    black.

We have lingered in the chambers of the sea
By sea-girls wreathed with seaweed red and
    brown
Till human voices wake us, and we drown.

—*T. S. Eliot*

On Time

Fly, envious Time, till thou run out thy race:
Call on the lazy leaden-stepping Hours,
Whose speed is but the heavy plummet`s pace;
And glut thyself with what thy womb devours,
Which is no more than what is false and vain,
And merely mortal dross;
So little is our loss,
So little is thy gain!
For, when as each thing bad thou hast
   entombed,
And, last of all, thy greedy Self consumed,
Then long eternity shall greet our bliss
With an individual kiss,
And joy shall undertake us as a flood;
When everything that is sincerely good
And perfectly divine,

With Truth, and Peace, and Love, shall ever
  shine
About the supreme Throne
Of Him, to whose happy-making sight alone
When once our heavenly-guided soul shall
  climb,
Then, all this earthly grossness quit,
Attired with stars we shall forever sit,
Triumphing over Death, and Chance, and thee,
O Time!

—*John Milton*

Peace

AH, that Time could touch a form
That could show what Homer's age
Bred to be a hero's wage.
"Were not all her life but storm
Would not painters paint a form
Of such noble lines,' I said,
"Such a delicate high head,
All that sternness amid charm,
All that sweetness amid strength?'
Ah, but peace that comes at length,
Came when Time had touched her form.

—W. B. Yeats

The Old Familiar Faces

I have had playmates, I have had companions
In my days of childhood, in my joyful
   schooldays;
  All, all are gone, the old familiar faces.

I have been laughing, I have been carousing,
Drinking late, sitting late, with my bosom
   cronies;
  All, all are gone, the old familiar faces.

I loved a love once, fairest among women:
Closed are her doors on me, I must not see
   her—
  All, all are gone, the old familiar faces.

I have a friend, a kinder friend has no man:
Like an ingrate, I left my friend abruptly;
  Left him, to muse on the old familiar faces.

Ghost-like I paced round the haunts of my
    childhood,
Earth seem'd a desert I was bound to traverse,
    Seeking to find the old familiar faces.

Friend of my bosom, thou more than a brother,
Why wert not thou born in my father's
    dwelling?
    So we might we talk of the old familiar
    faces—

How some they have died, and some they have
    left me,
And some are taken from me; all are
    departed—
    All, all are gone, the old familiar faces.

—*Charles Lamb*

To every thing there is a season

To every thing there is a season,
and a time to every purpose under the heaven:
A time to be born, a time to die;
a time to plant, and a time to pluck up that
   which is planted;
A time to kill, and a time to heal;
a time to break down, and a time to build up;
A time to weep, and a time to laugh;
a time to mourn, and a time to dance;
A time to cast away stones, and a time to gather
   stones together;
a time to embrace, and a time to refrain from
   embracing;
A time to get, and a time to lose;
a time to keep, and a time to cast away;
A time to rend, and a time to sew;
a time to keep silence, and a time to speak;

A time to love, and a time to hate;
A time of war, and a time of peace.

—*Ecclesiastes 3:18*

FAMILY AND
CHILDHOOD

Wynken, Blynken, and Nod

Wynken, Blynken, and Nod one night
    Sailed off in a wooden shoe,—
Sailed on a river of crystal light
    Into a sea of dew.
"Where are you going, and what do you
      wish?"
    The old moon asked the three.
"We have come to fish for the herring-fish
    That live in this beautiful sea;
    Nets of silver and gold have we,"
        Said Wynken,
        Blynken,
        And Nod.

The old moon laughed and sang a song,
    As they rocked in the wooden shoe;
And the wind that sped them all night long
    Ruffled the waves of dew;

The little stars were the herring-fish
    That lived in the beautiful sea.
"now cast your nets wherever you wish,—
    Never afeard are we!"
    So cried the stars to the fishermen three,
        Wynken,
        Blynken,
        And Nod.

All night long their nets they threw
    To the stars in the twinkling foam,—
Then down from the skies came the wooden
        shoe,
    Bringing the fishermen home:
'Twas all so pretty a sail, it seemed
    As if it could not be;
And some folk thought 'twas a dream they'd
        dreamed

Of sailing that beautiful sea;
But I shall name you the fishermen three:
    Wynken,
    Blynken,
    And Nod.

Wynken and Blynken are two little eyes,
  And Nod is a little head,
And the wooden shoe that sailed the skies
  Is a wee one's trundle-bed;
So shut your eyes while Mother sings
  Of wonderful sights that be,
And you shall see the beautiful things
  As you rock on the misty sea
  Where the old shoe rocked the fishermen
    three,—
    Wynken,
    Blynken,
    And Nod.

—*Eugene Field*

"Introduction" to
Songs of Innocence

Piping down the valleys wild,
Piping songs of pleasant glee,
On a cloud I saw a child,
And he laughing said to me:

"Pipe a song about a Lamb."
So I piped with merry cheer.
"Piper, pipe that song again."
So I piped; he wept to hear.

"Drop thy pipe, thy happy pipe;
Sing thy songs of happy cheer."
So I sung the same again
While he wept with joy to hear.

"Piper, sit thee down and write
In a book that all may read."
So he vanished from my sight,
And I plucked a hollow reed,

And I made a rural pen,
And I stained the water clear,
And I wrote my happy songs
Every child may joy to hear.

—*William Blake*

Home, Sweet Home

'Mid pleasures and palaces though we may
   roam,
Be it ever so humble, there's no place like
   home;
A charm from the sky sees to hallow us
   there,
Which, seek through the world, is ne'er met
   with elsewhere.
   Home, home, sweet, sweet home!
There's no place like home, oh, there's no
   place like home!

An exile from home, splendor dazzles in vain;
Oh, give me my lowly thatched cottage again!
The birds singing gaily, that came in my
   call—
Give me them—and the peace of mind,
   dearer than all!

Home, home, sweet, sweet home!
There's no place like home, oh, there's no
   place like home!

I gaze on the moon as I tread the drear wild,
And feel that my mother now thinks of her
   child,
As she looks on that moon from our own
   cottage door
Thro' the woodbine, whose fragrance shall
   cheer me no more.
   Home, home, sweet, sweet home!
There's no place like home, oh, there's no
   place like home!

How sweet 'tis to sit 'neath a fond father's
   smile,
And the caress of a mother to soothe and
   beguile!

Let others delight 'mid new pleasure to roam,
But give me, oh, give me, the pleasures of
    home,
    Home, home, sweet, sweet home!
There's no place like home, oh, there's no
    place like home!

To thee I'll return, overburdened with care;
The heart's dearest solace will smile on me
    there;
No more from that cottage again will I roam;
Be it ever so humble, there's no place like
    home.
    Home, home, sweet, sweet home!
There's no place like home, oh, there's no
    place like home!

—*John Howard Payne*

Mother o' Mine

If I were hanged on the highest hill,
　　Mother o' mine, O mother o' mine!
I know whose love would follow me still
　　Mother o' mine, O mother o' mine!
If I were drowned in the deepest sea,
　　Mother o' mine, O mother o' mine!
I know whose tears would come down to me,
　　Mother o' mine, O mother o' mine!
If I were damned by body and soul,
I know whose prayers would make me whole,
　　Mother o' mine, O mother o' mine!

—*Rudyard Kipling*

A Visit from Saint Nicholas

'Twas the night before Christmas, when all
   through the house
Not a creature was stirring, not even a mouse;
The stockings were hung by the chimney
   with care,
In hopes that St. Nicholas soon would be
   there;
The children were nestled all snug in their
   beds,
While visions of sugar-plums danced in their
   heads;
And mamma in her kerchief, and I in my cap,
Had just settled our brains for a long winter's
   nap,
When out on the lawn these arose such a
   clatter,
I sprang from the bed to see what was the
   matter.

Away to the window I flew like a flash,
Tore open the shutters, and threw up the
  sash.
The moon on the breast of the new-fallen
  snow
Gave a luster of mid-day to objects below,
When, what to my wondering eyes should
  appear,
But a miniature sleigh, and eight tiny
  reindeer,
With a little old driver, so lively and quick,
I knew in a moment it must be St. Nick.
More rapid than eagles his courses they
  came,
And he whistled, and shouted, and called
  them by name;
"Now, *Dasher!* now, *Dancer!* now, *Prancer*
  and *Vixen!*

On, *Comet!* on, *Cupid!* on *Donner*, and
    Blitzen!
To the top of the porch! To the top of the
    wall!
Now, dash away! Dash away! Dash away all!"
As dry leaves that before the wild hurricane
    fly,
When they meet with an obstacle, mount to
    the sky;
So up to the housetop the coursers they flew,
With the sleigh full of toys, and St. Nicholas,
    too.
And then in a twinkling, I heard on the roof
The prancing and pawing of each little hoof.
As I drew in my head, and was turning
    around,
Down the chimney St. Nicholas came with a
    bound.

He was dressed all in fur, from his head to his
    foot,
And his clothes were all tarnished with ashes
    and soot;
A bundle of toys he had flung on his back,
And he looked like a peddler just opening his
    pack.
His eyes—how they twinkled!—his dimples
    how merry!
His cheeks were like roses, his nose like a
    cherry!
His droll little mouth was drawn up like a
    bow,
And the beard of his chin was as white as the
    snow;
The stump of a pipe he held tight in his teeth,
And the smoke it encircled his head like a
    wreath;

He had a broad face and a round little belly,
That shook when he laughed like a bowlful of
    jelly.
He was chubby and plump, a right jolly old
    elf,
And I laughed when I saw him, in spite of
    myself;
A wink of his eye and a twist of his head,
Soon gave me to know I had nothing to
    dread;
He spoke not a word, but went straight to his
    work,
And filled all the stockings; then turned with
    a jerk;
And laying his finger aside of his nose,
And giving a nod, up the chimney he rose;
He sprang to his sleigh, to his team gave a
    whistle,

And away they all flew like the down of a
   thistle;
But I heard him exclaim, ere he drove out of
   sight,
"Happy Christmas to all, and to all a good
   night!"

—*Clement Moore*

The Children's Hour

Between the dark and the daylight,
   When the night is beginning to lower,
Comes a pause in the day's occupations,
   That is known as the Children's Hour.

I hear in the chamber above me
   The patter of little feet,
The sound of a door that is opened,
   And voices soft and sweet.

From my study I see in the lamplight,
   Descending the broad hall stair,
Grave Alice, and laughing Allegra,
   And Edith with golden hair.

A whisper, and then a silence:
   Yet I know by their merry eyes
They are plotting and planning together
   To take me by surprise.

A sudden rush from the stairway,
  A sudden raid from the hall!
By three doors left unguarded
  They enter my castle wall!

They climb up into my turret
  O'er the arms and back of my chair;
If I try to escape, they surround me;
  They seem to be everywhere.

They almost devour me with kisses,
  Their arms about me entwine,
Till I think of the Bishop of Bingen
  In his Mouse-Tower on the Rhine!

Do you think, O blue-eyed banditti,
  Because you have scaled the wall,
Such an old mustache as I am
  Is not a match for you all!

I have you fast in my fortress,
  And will not let you depart,
But put you down into the dungeon
  In the round-tower of my heart.

And there will I keep you forever,
  Yes, forever and a day,
Till the walls shall crumble to ruin,
  And moulder in dust away.

—*Henry Wadsworth Longfellow*

Children

Monday's child is fair of face,
Tuesday's child is full of grace,
Wednesday's child is full of woe,
Thursdays' child has far to go,
Friday's child is loving and giving,
Saturday's child works hard for his living,
And the child that is born on the Sabbath day
Is bonny and blithe, and good and gay.

—*Anonymous*

The Sugar-Plum Tree

Have you ever heard of the Sugar-Plum Tree?
   'Tis a marvel of great renown!
It blooms on the shore of the Lollipop sea
   In the garden of Shut-Eye Town;
The fruit that it bears is so wondrously sweet
   (As those who have tasted it say)
That good little children have only to eat
   Of that fruit to be happy next day.

When you've got to the tree, you would have
   a hard time
   To capture the fruit which I sing;
The tree is so tall that no person could climb
   To the boughs where the sugar-plums
   swing!
But up in that tree sits a chocolate cat,
   And a gingerbread dog prowls below—
And this is the way you contrive to get at
   Those sugar-plums tempting you so:

You say but the word to that gingerbread dog
    And he barks with such terrible zest
That the chocolate cat is at once all agog,
    As her swelling proportions attest.
And the chocolate cat goes cavorting around
    From this leafy limb unto that,
And the sugar-plums tumble, of course, to the
        ground—
    Hurrah for that chocolate cat!

There are marshmallows, gumdrops, and
        peppermint canes,
    With stripings of scarlet or gold,
And you carry away of the treasure that rains
    As much as your apron can hold!
So come, little child, cuddle closer to me
    In your dainty white nightcap and gown,
And I'll rock you away to that Sugar-Plum Tree
    In the garden of Shut-Eye Town.

—*Eugene Field*

There Was a Little Girl

There was a little girl, she had a little curl
  Right in the middle of her forehead;
And when she was good, she was very, very
    good,
And when she was bad, she was horrid.

—*Henry Wadsworth Longfellow*

Baby Charley

He's fast asleep.   See how, O Wife,
Night's finger on the lip of life
Bids whist the tongue, so prattle-rife,
    Of busy Baby Charley.

One arm stretched backward round his head,
Five little toes from out the bed
Just showing, like five rosebuds red,
—So slumbers Baby Charley.

Heaven-lights, I know, are beaming through
Those lucent eyelids, veined with blue,
That shut away from mortal view
    Large eyes of Baby Charley.

O sweet Sleep-Angel, throned now
On the round glory of his brow,
Wave thy wing and waft my vow
    Breathed over Baby Charley.

I vow that my heart, when death is nigh,
Shall never shiver with a sigh
For act of hand or tongue or eye
    That wronged my Baby Charley!

—*Sidney Lanier*

Cradle Song

What does little birdie say
In her nest at peep of day?
Let me fly, says little birdie,
Mother, let me fly away.
Birdie, rest a little longer,
Till thy little wings are stronger.
So she rests a little longer,
Then she flies away.

What does little baby say,
In her bed at peep of day?
Baby says, like little birdie,
Let me rise and fly away.
Baby, sleep a little longer,
Till thy little limbs are stronger.
If she sleeps a little longer,
Baby too shall fly away.

—*Alfred, Lord Tennyson*

Lullaby

Golden slumbers kiss your eyes,
Smiles awake you when you rise.
Sleep, pretty wantons; do not cry,
And I will sing a lullaby:
Rock them, rock them, lullaby.

Care is heavy, therefore sleep you;
You are care, and care must keep you.
Sleep, pretty wantons; do not cry,
And I will sing a lullaby:
Rock them, rock them, lullaby.

—*Thomas Dekker*

The Old Oaken Bucket

How dear to my heart are the scenes of my
    childhood,
  When fond recollection presents them to
    view!
The orchard, the meadow, the deep-tangled
    wildwood,
  And every loved spot which my infancy
    knew,
The wide-spreading pond and the mill which
    stood by it,
  The bridge and the rock where the cataract
    fell;
The cot of my father, the dairy house nigh it,
  And e'en the rude-bucket which hung in
    the well.
The old oaken bucket, the iron-bound bucket,
The moss-covered bucket which hung in the
    well.

That moss-covered vessel I hail as a treasure;
  For often at noon, when returned from the
    field,
I found it the source of an exquisite pleasure,
  The purest and sweetest that nature can
    yield.
How ardent I seized it with hands that were
    glowing!
  And quick to the white-pebbled bottom it
    fell;
Then soon, with the emblem of truth
    overflowing,
  And dripping with coolness it rose from the
    well;
The old oaken bucket, the iron-bound bucket,
The moss-covered bucket, arose from the
    well.

How sweet form the green mossy brim to
    receive it,
  As poised on the curb, it inclined to me
    lips!
Not a full blushing goblet could tempt me to
    leave it,
  Though filled with the nectar that Jupiter
    sips.
And now, far removed from the loved
    situation,
  The tear of regret will intrusively swell,
As fancy reverts to my father's plantation,
  And sighs for the bucket which hangs in
    the well;
The old oaken bucket, the iron-bound bucket,
The moss-covered bucket which hangs in the
    well.

—*Samuel Woodworth*

Prayer for My Daughter

Once more the storm is howling, and half hid
Under this cradle-hood and coverlid
My child sleeps on. There is no obstacle
But Gregory's wood and one bare hill
Whereby the haystack- and roof-levelling wind,
Bred on the Atlantic, can be stayed;
And for an hour I have walked and prayed
Because of the great gloom that is in my mind.

I have walked and prayed for this young child
   an hour
And heard the sea-wind scream upon the tower,
And under the arches of the bridge, and scream
In the elms above the flooded stream;
Imagining in excited reverie
That the future years had come,
Dancing to a frenzied drum,
Out of the murderous innocence of the sea.

May she be granted beauty and yet not
Beauty to make a stranger's eye distraught,
Or hers before a looking-glass, for such,
Being made beautiful overmuch,
Consider beauty a sufficient end,
Lose natural kindness and maybe
The heart-revealing intimacy
That chooses right, and never find a friend.

Helen being chosen found life flat and dull
And later had much trouble from a fool,
While that great Queen, that rose out of the
    spray,
Being fatherless could have her way
Yet chose a bandy-leggèd smith for man.
It's certain that fine women eat
A crazy salad with their meat
Whereby the Horn of Plenty is undone.

In courtesy I'd have her chiefly learned;
Hearts are not had as a gift but hearts are
  earned
By those that are not entirely beautiful;
Yet many, that have played the fool
For beauty's very self, has charm made wise,
And many a poor man that has roved,
Loved and thought himself beloved,
From a glad kindness cannot take his eyes.

May she become a flourishing hidden tree
That all her thoughts may like the linnet be,
And have no business but dispensing round
Their magnanimities of sound,
Nor but in merriment begin a chase,
Nor but in merriment a quarrel.
O may she live like some green laurel
Rooted in one dear perpetual place.

My mind, because the minds that I have loved,
The sort of beauty that I have approved,
Prosper but little, has dried up of late,
Yet knows that to be choked with hate
May well be of all evil chances chief.
If there's no hatred in a mind
Assault and battery of the wind
Can never tear the linnet from the leaf.

An intellectual hatred is the worst,
So let her think opinions are accursed.
Have I not seen the loveliest woman born
Out of the mouth of Plenty's horn,
Because of her opinionated mind
Barter that horn and every good
By quiet natures understood
For an old bellows full of angry wind?

Considering that, all hatred driven hence,
The soul recovers radical innocence
And learns at last that it is self-delighting,
Self-appeasing, self-affrighting,
And that its own sweet will is Heaven's will;
She can, though every face should scowl
And every windy quarter howl
Or every bellows burst, be happy still.

And may her bridegroom bring her to a house
Where all's accustomed, ceremonious;
For arrogance and hatred are the wares
Peddled in the thoroughfares.
How but in custom and in ceremony
Are innocence and beauty born?
Ceremony's a name for the rich horn,
And custom for the spreading laurel tree.

—*W. B. Yeats*

Childhood

HOW I could see through and through you!
So unconscious, tender, kind,
More than ever was known to you
Of the pure ways of your mind.

We who long to rest from strife
Labour sternly as a duty;
But a magic in your life
Charms, unknowing of its beauty.

We are pools whose depths are told;
You are like a mystic fountain,
Issuing ever pure and cold
From the hollows of the mountain.

We are men by anguish taught
To distinguish false from true;
Higher wisdom we have not;
But a joy within guides you.

—*George William ("A. E.") Russell*

Childhood

It would be good to give much thought, before
you try to find words for something so lost,
for those long childhood afternoons you knew
that vanished so completely—and why?

We're still reminded—: sometimes by a rain,
but we can no longer say what it means;
life was never again so filled with meeting,
with reunion and with passing on

as back then, when nothing happened to us
except what happens to things and creatures:
we lived their world as something human,
and became filled to the brim with figures.

And became as lonely as a shepherd
and as overburdened by vast distances,
and summoned and stirred as from far away,

and slowly, like a long new thread,
introduced into that picture-sequence
where now having to go on bewilders us.

—*Rainer Maria Rilke*
(Translated by Edward Snow)

Odysseus to Telemachus

My dear Telemachus,
The Trojan War
Is over now; I don't recall who won it.
The Greeks, no doubt, for only they would
   leave
so many dead so far from their own homeland.
But still, my homeward way has proved too
   long.
While we were wasting time there, old
   Poseidon,
it almost seems, stretched and extended space.

I don't know where I am or what this place
can be. It would appear some filthy island,
with bushes, buildings, and great grunting pigs.
A garden choked with weeds; some queen or
   other.
Grass and huge stones...Telemachus, my son!

To a wanderer the faces of all islands
Resemble one another. And the mind
trips, numbering waves; eyes, sore from sea
    horizons,
run; and the flesh of water stuffs the ears.
I can't remember how the war came out;
even how old are you—I can't remember.

Grow up, then, my Telemachus, grow strong.
Only the gods know if we'll see each other
again. You've long since ceased to be that babe
before whom I reined in the plowing bullocks.
Had it not been for Palamedes' trick
we two would still be living in one household.
But maybe he was right; away from me
you are quite safe from all Oedipal passions,
and your dreams, my Telemachus, are blameless.

—*Joseph Brodsky*

The Lanyard

The other day as I was ricocheting slowly
off the blue walls of this room,
moving as if underwater from typewriter to
   piano,
from bookshelf to an envelope lying on the
   floor,
when I found myself moving as if underwater
in the L section of the dictionary
where my eyes fell upon the word lanyard.

No cookie nibbled by a French novelist
could send one into the past more suddenly—
a past where I sat at a workbench at a camp
by a deep Adirondack lake
learning how to braid thin plastic strips
into a lanyard, a gift for my mother.

I had never seen anyone use a lanyard
or wear one, if that's what you did with them,
but that did not keep me from crossing
strand over strand again and again
until I had made a boxy
red and white lanyard for my mother.

She gave me life and milk from her breasts
and I in turn, presented her with a lanyard.
She nursed me in many a sick room,
lifted spoons of medicine to my lips,
laid cold face cloths on my forehead,
then led me out into the airy light
and taught me to walk and swim,
and I, in turn, presented her with a lanyard.

Here are thousands of meals, she said,
and here is clothing and a good education.

And here is your lanyard, I replied,
which I made with a little help from a counselor.

Here is a breathing body and a beating heart,
strong legs, bones and teeth,
and two clear eyes to read the world, she
    whispered,
and here, I said, is the lanyard I made at camp.
And here, I wish to say to her now,
is a smaller gift—
not the worn truth
that you can never repay your mother,
but the rueful admission that when she took
the two-toned lanyard from my hand,
I was as sure as a boy could be
that this useless, worthless thing I wove
out of boredom would be enough to make us
    even.

—Billy Collins

My Wicked, Wicked Ways

This is my father.
See? He is young.
He looks like Errol Flynn.
He is wearing a hat
that tips over one eye,
a suit that fits him good,
and baggy pants.
He is also wearing
those awful shoes,
the two-toned ones
my mother hates.

Here is my mother.
She is not crying.
She cannot look into the lens
because the sun is bright.
The woman,
the one my father knows,
is not here.
She does not come till later.

My mother will get very mad.
Her face will turn red
and she will throw one shoe.
My father will say nothing.
After a while everyone
will forget it.
Years and years will pass.

My mother will stop mentioning it.
This is me she is carrying.
I am a baby.
She does not know
I will turn out bad.

—*Sandra Cisneros*

FAITH AND
SPIRITUALITY

Some Keep the Sabbath Going to Church

Some keep the Sabbath going to Church—
I keep it, staying at Home—
With a Bobolink for a Chorister—
And an Orchard, for a Dome—

Some keep the Sabbath in Surplice—
I just wear my Wings—
And instead of tolling the Bell, for Church,
Out little Sexton—sings.

God preaches, a noted Clergyman—
And the sermon is never long,
So instead of getting to Heaven, at last—
I'm going, all along.

—*Emily Dickinson*

My Heart Leaps Up When I Behold

My heart leaps up when I behold
  A rainbow in the sky;
So was it when my life began;
So is it now I am a man;
So be it when I shall grow old,
  Or let me die!
The Child is father of the Man;
And I could wish my days to be
Bound each to each by natural piety.

—*William Wordsworth*

Remember

Remember me when I am gone away,
   Gone far away into the silent land;
   When you can no more hold me by the
     hand,
Nor I half turn to go yet turning stay.
Remember me when no more day by day
   You tell me of our future that you planned:
   Only remember me; you understand
It will be late to counsel then or pray.
Yet if you should forget me for a while
   And afterwards remember, do not grieve:
   For if the darkness and corruption leave
   A vestige of the thoughts that once I had,
Better by far you should forget and smile
   Than that you should remember and be
     sad.

—*Christina Georgina Rossetti*

In Flanders Fields

In Flanders fields the poppies blow
Between the crosses, row on row,
   That mark our place; and in the sky
   The larks, still bravely singing, fly
Scarce heard amid the guns below.

We are the Dead. Short days ago
We lived, felt dawn, saw sunset glow,
   Loved and were loved, and now we lie
   In Flanders fields.

Take up out quarrel with the foe:
To you from failing hands we throw
   The torch; be yours to hold it high.
   If ye break faith with us who die
We shall not sleep, though poppies grow
   In Flanders fields.

—*John McCrae*

Prospice

Fear death?—to feel the fog in my throat,
    The mist in my face,
When the snows begin, and the blasts denote
    I am nearing the place,
The power of the night, the press of the storm,
    The post of the foe;
Where he stands, the Arch Fear in a visible
      form,
    Yet the strong man must go:
For the journey is done and the summit
      attained,
    And the barriers fall,
Though a battle's to fight ere the guerdon be
      gained,
    The reward of it all.
I was ever a fighter, so—one fight more,
    The best and the last!
I would hate that death bandaged my eyes,
      and forbore,
    And bade me creep past,

No! let me taste the whole of it, fare like my
    peers
  The heroes of old,
Bear the brunt, in a minute pay glad life's
    arrears
  Of pain, darkness and cold.
For sudden the worst turns the best to the
    brave,
  The black minute's at end,
And the element's rage, the fiend-voices that
    rave,
  Shall dwindle, shall blend,
Shall change, shall become first a peace out of
    pain,
  Then a light, then thy breast,
O thou soul of my soul! I shall clasp thee
    again,
  And with God be the rest!

—*Robert Browning*

After Great Pain, a Formal Feeling Comes

After great pain, a formal feeling comes—
The Nerves sit ceremonious, like Tombs—
The stiff Heart questions was it He, that bore,
And Yesterday, or Centuries before?

The Feet, mechanical, go round—
Of Ground, or Air, or Ought—
A Wooden way
Regardless grown,
A Quartz contentment, like a stone—

This is the Hour of Lead—
Remembered, if outlived,
As Freezing persons, recollect the Snow—
First—Chill—then Stupor—then the letting
  go—

—*Emily Dickinson*

The Road Not Taken

Two roads diverged in a yellow wood,
And sorry I could not travel both
And be one traveler, long I stood
And looked down one as far as I could
To where it bent in the undergrowth;

Then took the other, as just as fair,
And having perhaps the better claim,
Because it was grassy and wanted wear;
Though as for that the passing there
Had worn them really about the same,

And both that morning equally lay
In leaves no step had trodden black.
Oh, I kept the first for another day!
Yet knowing how way leads on to way,
I doubted if I should ever come back.

I shall be telling this with a sigh
Somewhere ages and ages hence:
Two roads diverged in a wood, and I—
I took the one less traveled by,
And that has made all the difference.

—*Robert Frost*

The Lamb

Little Lamb, who made thee?
Dost thou know who made thee?
Gave thee life, and bid thee feed
By the stream and o'er the mead;
Gave thee clothing of delight,
Softest clothing, woolly, bright;
Gave thee such a tender voice,
Making all the vales rejoice?
Little Lamb, who made thee?
Dost thou know who made thee?
Little Lamb, I'll tell thee,
Little Lamb, I'll tell thee:
He is callèd by thy name,
For he calls himself a Lamb,
His is meek, and he is mild;
He became a little child.
I a child, and thou a lamb.
We are callèd by his name.
Little Lamb, God bless thee!
Little Lamb, God bless thee!

—*William Blake*

When I Have Fears That I May Cease to Be

When I have fears that I may cease to be
   Before my pen has gleaned my teeming
      brain,
Before high-pilèd books, in charactry,
   Hold like rich garners the full ripen'd grain;
When I behold, upon the night's starr'd face,
   Huge cloudy symbols of a high romance,
And I think that I may never live to trace
   Their shadows, with the magic hand of
      chance;
And when I feel, fair creature of an hour!
   That I shall never look upon thee more,
Never have relish in the faery power
   Of unreflecting love;—then on the shore
Of the wide world I stand alone, and think
Till Love and Fame to nothingness do sink.

—*John Keats*

If—

If you can keep you head when all about you
   Are losing theirs and blaming it on you;
If you can trust yourself when all men doubt
     you,
   But make allowance for their doubting too;
If you can wait and not be tired by waiting,
   Or, being lied about, don't deal in lies,
Or, being hated, don't give way to hating,
   And yet don't look too good, nor talk too
     wise;

* * *

If you can dream—and not make dreams
     your master;
   If you can think—and not make thoughts
     your aim;
If you can meet with triumph and disaster
   And treat those two impostors just the
     same;

If you can bear to hear the truth you've
     spoken
   Twisted by knaves to make a trap for fools,
Or watch the things you gave your life to
     broken,
   And stood and build 'em up with worn out
     tools;

If you can make one heap of all your
     winnings
   And risk it on one turn of pitch-and-toss,
And lost, and start again at your beginnings
   And never breathe a word about your loss;
If you can force your heart and nerve and
     sinew
   To serve your turn long after they are gone,
And so hold on when there is nothing in you
   Except the Will which says to them: "Hold
     on";

*   *   *

If you can talk with crowds and keep your
    virtue,
  Or walk with kings—nor lose the common
      touch;
If neither foes nor loving friends can hurt
    you;
  If all men count with you, but none too
    much;
If you can fill the unforgiving minute
  With sixty seconds' worth of distance run—
Yours is the Earth and everything that's in it,
  And—which is more—you'll be a Man, my
    son!

—*Rudyard Kipling*

Ode on Solitude

Happy the man, whose wish and care
  A few paternal acres bound,
Content to breathe his native air,
     In his own ground.

Whose herds with milk, whose fields with
     bread,
  Whose flocks supply him with attire,
Whose trees in summer yield him shade,
     In winter fire.

Blest, who can unconcern'dly find
  Hours, days, and years slide soft away,
In health of body, peace of mind,
     Quiet by day,

Sound sleep by night; study and ease,
    Together mixt; sweet recreation;
And innocence, which most does please
        With meditation.

Thus let me live, unseen, unknown;
    Thus unlamented let me die;
Steal from the world, and not a stone
        Tell where I lie.

—*Alexander Pope*

Up-Hill

Does the road wind up-hill all the way?
  Yes, to the very end.
Will the day's journey take the whole long
    day?
  From morn to night, my friend.

But is there for the night a resting-place?
  A roof for when the slow dark hours begin.
May not the darkness hide it from my face?
  You cannot miss that inn.

Shall I meet other wayfarers at night?
  Those who have gone before.
Then must I knock, or call when just in sight?
  *They will not keep you standing at that
    door.*

Shall I find comfort, travel-sore and weak?
　　Of labour you shall find the sum.
Will there be beds for me and all who seek?
　　Yea, beds for all who come.

—*Christina Georgina Rossetti*

Rock of Ages

Rock of Ages, cleft for me,
Let me hide myself in Thee!
Let the water and the blood,
From Thy riven side which flow'd,
Be of sin the double cure,
Cleanse me from its guilt and power.

Not the labors of my hands
Can fulfil Thy law's demands;
Could my zeal no respite know,
Could my tears forever flow,
All for sin could not atone;
Thou must save, and Thou alone.

Nothing in my hand I bring;
Simply to Thy Cross I cling;
Naked, come to Thee for dress;
Helpless, look to Thee for grace;
Foul, I to the Fountain fly;
Wash me, Saviour, or I die!

While I draw this fleeting breath,
When my eyestrings break in death,
When I soar through tracts unknown,
See Thee on Thy judgment-throne;
Rock of Ages, cleft for me,
Let me hide myself in Thee!

—*Augustus Montague Toplady*

The Pilgrimage

Give me my scallop-shell of quiet,
  My staff of faith to walk upon.
My scrip of joy, immortal diet,
  My bottle of salvation,
My gown of glory, hope's true gage;
And thus I'll take my pilgrimage.

Blood must be my body's balmer;
  No this balm will there be given;
Whilst my soul, like quiet palmer,
  Travelleth towards the land of heaven;
Over the silver mountains,
Where spring the nectar fountains;
  There will I kiss
  The bowll of bliss;
  And drink mine everlasting fuill
  Upon every milken hill,
  My soul will be a-dry before;
  But, after, it will thirst no more.

—*Sir Walter Raleigh*

Pax

All that matters is to be at one with the living
 God
To be a creature in the house of the God of Life

Like a cat asleep on a chair
At peace, in peace
And at one with the master of the house, with
 the mistress,
At home, at home in the house of the living,
Sleeping on the hearth, and yawning before the
 fire.

Sleeping on the hearth of the living world
Yawning at home before the fire of life
Feeling the presence of the living God
Like a great reassurance
A deep calm in the heart
A presence

As of the master sitting at the board
In his own and greater being,
In the house of Life.

—*D. H. Lawrence*

"I Have a Rendezvous with Death"

I have a rendezvous with Death
At some disputed barricade,
When Spring comes back with rustling shade
And apple-blossoms fill the air—
I have a rendezvous with Death
When Spring brings back blue days and fair.

It may be he shall take my hand
And lead me into his dark land
And close my eyes and quench my breath—
It may be I shall pass him still.
I have a rendezvous with Death
On some scarred slope of battered hill,
When Spring comes round again this year
And the first meadow-flowers appear.

God knows 'twere better to be deep
Pillowed in silk and scented down,
Where Love throbs out in blissful sleep,
Pulse night to pulse, and breath to breath,
Where hushed awakenings are dear . . .
But I've a rendezvous with Death
At midnight in some flaming town,
When Spring trips north again this year,
And I to my pledged word am true,
I shall not fail that rendezvous.

—*Alan Seeger*

When I Heard the Learn'd Astronomer

When I heard the learn'd astronomer,
When the proofs, the figures, were ranged in
    columns before me,
When I was shown the charts and diagrams,
    to add, divide, and measure them
When I sitting heard the astronomer where
    he lectured with much applause in the
    lecture-room,
How soon unaccountable I became tired and
    sick,
Till rising and gliding out I wander'd off by
    myself,
In the mystical moist night air, and from time
    to time,
Look'd up in perfect silence at the stars.

—*Walt Whitman*

Death Be Not Proud

Death be not proud, though some have
  called thee
Mighty and dreadful, for thou art not so,
For those, whom thou thinkest thou dost
  overthrow,
Die not, poor death, nor yet canst thou kill
  me.
From rest and sleep, which but thy pictures
  be,
Much pleasure, then from thee much more
  must flow,
And soonest our best men with thee do go,
Rest of their bones and soul's delivery.
Thou art slave to Fate, chance, kings and
  desperate men,
And dost with poison, war, and sickness
  dwell,

And poppy or charms can make us sleep as
   well
And better than thy stroke; why swellest thou
   then?
One short sleep past, we wake eternally,
And death shall be no more; Death thou shalt
   die.

—*John Donne*

Requiem

Under the wide and starry sky
Dig the grave and let me lie.
Glad did I live and gladly die,
    And I laid me down with a will.

This be the verse you grave for me:
Here he lies where he longed to be;
Home is the sailor, home from sea,
    And the hunter home from the hill.

—*Robert Louis Stevenson*

Sometimes I Feel Like a Motherless Child

Sometimes I feel like a motherless child,
Sometimes I feel like a motherless child,
Sometimes I feel like a motherless child,
A long ways from home,
A long way from home.
True believer,
A long ways from home.
A long way from home.

Sometimes I feel like I'm almost gone,
Sometimes I feel like I'm almost gone,
Sometimes I feel like I'm almost gone,
Way up in the heavenly land,
Way up in the heavenly land.
True believer,
Way up in the heavenly land,
Way up in the heavenly land.

Sometimes I feel like a motherless child,
Sometimes I feel like a motherless child,
Sometimes I feel like a motherless child,
A long ways from home,
A long way from home.
True believer,
A long ways from home.
A long way from home.

—*Anonymous*

In Church

In the choir the boys are singing the hymn.
  The morning light on their lips
Moves in silver-moist flashes, in musical trim.

Sudden outside the high window, one crow
  Hangs in the air
And lights on a withered oak-tree's top of woe.

One bird, one blot, folded and still at the top
  Of the withered tree!—in the grail
Of crystal heaven falls one full black drop.

Life a soft full drop of darkness it seems to sway
  In the tender wine
Of our Sabbath, suffusing our sacred day.

—*D. H. Lawrence*

Annabel Lee

It was many and many a year ago,
  In a kingdom by the sea,
That a maiden there lived whom you may know
  By the name of Annabel Lee;
And this maiden she lived with no other
  thought
  Than to love and be loved by me.

I was a child and *she* was a child,
  In this kingdom by the sea:
But we loved with a love that was more than
  love—
  I and my Annabel Lee;
With a love that the winged seraphs of heaven
  Coveted her and me.

And this was the reason that, long ago,
  In this kingdom by the sea,

A wind blew out of a cloud, chilling
   My beautiful Annabel Lee;
So that her highborn kinsman came
   And bore her away from me,
To shut her up in a sepulchre
   In this kingdom by the sea.

The angels, not half so happy in heaven,
   Went envying her and me—
Yes!—that was the reason (as all men know,
   In this kingdom by the sea)
That the wind came out of the cloud by night,
   Chilling and killing my Annabel Lee.

But our love it was stronger by far than the love
   Of those who were older than we—
   Of many far wiser than we—

And neither the angels in heaven above,
  Nor the demons down under the sea,
Can ever dissever my soul from the soul
  Of the beautiful Annabel Lee:

For the moon never beams, without bringing me
dreams
  Of the beautiful Annabel Lee;
And the stars never rise, but I feel the bright
  eyes
  Of the beautiful Annabel Lee;
And so, all the night-tide, I lie down by the side
  Of my darling—my darling—my life and my
  bride,
  In her sepulchre there by the sea,
  In her tomb by the sounding sea.

—*Edgar Allan Poe*

De Chu'ch

'Way down de lane, behin' a row o' trees,
Whaih all de summah croons de softes' breeze
De ol' plantashun chu'ch am shinin' white.
We da'kies lingah daih each Sund'y night,
A-shoutin' praise to Gawd an' Jesus, too.
We love de benches, made o' pine tree wood,
We love de place whaih all de elduhs stood
Each qua'tly meetin' day, a singin' himes
An' tellin' us erbout de good ol' times
W'en 'ligion was de only thing on earf.
De preachuh's haid widout an inch o' turf
Went waggin' 'way lak he's b'en set on fiah
"O Chillun, in de hebben libs de quiah
Ob dose who shaired de trubbles ob de Lawd,
Ob dose who found below de love ob Gawd.
Come throw yo' se'f befo' de Mussy Seat,
Come wash in Jesus blood yo' sinful feet.
De Son ob Man's de Shephud ob de fol',
De cripple lain' beneaf His cloak He hol'.

In Hebben He hab filled yo' honey dish,
Yo' comin' homewa'd's all dat He kin wish."
He hug de bible, an' de sistahs shout
A-puttin' all de debbils to de rout,
"Ol' Mount Moriah's lifted to de sky
An' anguls on de wing go flittin' by."
But w'en de deacon pass de wine an' braid
Each Christ'un soul in reverence hang his haid.
He am de chosen brothah ob de King,
An' low an' mounful lak he's sho' to sing,
"Ah want to meet mah Saviour face to face."
No, honey! all de worl' kin hol' no place

Jes' lak de ol' plantsshun chu'ch ob mine;
It am de manshun ob de lowly folk,
It am de spot whaih Gawd Himself hab spoke,
It am de only place to shake de han',
An' know flat you's as good as any man.
Oh, dat's de place fu' me to live an' die,
Benear de Mussy ob de Saviour's eye.

—*Fenton Johnson*

God's World

O WORLD, I cannot hold thee close enough!
Thy winds, thy wide grey skies!
Thy mists, that roll and rise!
Thy woods, this autumn day, that ache and sag
And all but cry with colour! That gaunt crag
To crush! To lift the lean of that black bluff!
World, World, I cannot get thee close enough!
Long have I known a glory in it all,
But never knew I this;
Here such a passion is
As stretcheth me apart,—Lord, I do fear
Thou'st made the world too beautiful this year;
My soul is all but out of me,—let fall
No burning leaf; prithee, let no bird call.

—*Edna St. Vincent Millay*

Heaven

Fish (fly-replete, in depth of June,
Dawdling away their wat'ry noon)
Ponder deep wisdom, dark or clear,
Each secret fishy hope or fear.
Fish say, they have their Stream and Pond;
But is there anything Beyond?
This life cannot be All, they swear,
For how unpleasant, if it were!
One may not doubt that, somehow, Good
Shall come of Water and of Mud;
And, sure, the reverent eye must see
A Purpose in Liquidity.
We darkly know, by Faith we cry,
The future is not Wholly Dry.
Mud unto mud!—Death eddies near—
Not here the appointed End, not here!
But somewhere, beyond Space and Time.
Is wetter water, slimier slime!

And there (they trust) there swimmeth One
Who swam ere rivers were begun,
Immense, of fishy form and mind,
Squamous, omnipotent, and kind;
And under that Almighty Fin,
The littlest fish may enter in.
Oh! never fly conceals a hook,
Fish say, in the Eternal Brook,
But more than mundane weeds are there,
And mud, celestially fair;
Fat caterpillars drift around,
And Paradisal grubs are found;
Unfading moths, immortal flies,
And the worm that never dies.
And in that Heaven of all their wish,
There shall be no more land, say fish.

—*Rupert Brooke*

A Prayer on Going into My House

God grant a blessing on this tower and cottage
And on my heirs, if all remain unspoiled.
No table, or chair or stool not simple enough
For shepherd lads in Galilee; and grant
That I myself for portions of the year
May handle nothing and set eyes on nothing
But what the great and passionate have used
Throughout so many varying centuries
We take it for the norm; yet should I dream
Sinbad the sailor's brought a painted chest
Or image, from beyond the Loadstone Mountain;
That dream is a norm; and should some limb of
    the devil
Destroy the view by cutting down an ash
That shades the road, or setting up a cottage
Planned in a government office, shorten his life,
Manacle his soul upon the Red Sea bottom.

—*W. B. Yeats*

WIT AND HUMOR

The Walrus and
the Carpenter

The sun was shining on the sea,
    Shining with all his might:
He did his very best to make
    The billows smooth and bright—
And this was odd, because it was
    The middle of the night.

The moon was shining sulkily,
    Because she thought the sun
Had got no business to be there
    After the day was done—
"It's very rude of him," she said,
    "To come and spoil the fun!"

The sea was wet as wet could be,
    The sands were dry as dry.
You could not see a could, because
    No cloud was in the sky:
No birds were flying overhead
    There were no birds to fly.

The Walrus and the Carpenter
 Were walking close at hand:
They wept like anything to see
 Such quantities of sand.
"If this were only cleared away,"
 They said, "it would be grand!"

"If seven maids with seven mops
 Swept it for half a year,
Do you suppose," the Walrus said,
 "That they could get it clear?"
"I doubt it," said the Carpenter,
 And shed a bitter tear.

"O Oysters, come and walk with us!"
 The Walrus did beseech.
"A pleasant walk, a pleasant talk,
 Along the briny beach:
We cannot do with more than four,
 To give a hand to each."

The eldest Oyster looked at him,
  But never a word he said:
The eldest Oyster winked his eye,
  And shook his heavy head—
Meaning to say he did not choose
  To leave the oyster-bed.

But four young Oysters hurried up,
  All eager for the treat:
Their coats were brushed, their faces washed,
  Their shoes were clean and neat—
And this was odd, because, you know,
  They hadn't any feet.

Four other Oysters followed them
  And yet another four;
And thick and fast they came at last,
  And more, and more, and more—
All hopping through the frothy waves,
  And scrambling to the shore.

The Walrus and the Carpenter
   Walked on a mile or so,
And then they rested on a rock
   Conveniently low:
And all the little Oysters stood
   And waited in a row.

"The time has come," the Walrus said,
   "To talk of many things:
Of shoes—and ships—and scaling wax—
   Of cabbages—and kings—
And why the sea is boiling hot—
   And whether pigs have wings."

"But wait a bit," the Oysters cried,
   "Before we have our chat;
For some of us are out of breath,
   And all of us are fat!"
"No hurry!" said the Carpenter.
   They thanked him much for that.

"A loaf of bread," the Walrus said,
    "Is what we chiefly need:
Pepper and vinegar besides
    Are very good indeed—
Now, if you're ready, Oysters dear,
    We can begin to feed."

"But not on us!" the Oysters cried,
    Turning a little blue.
"After such kindness, that would be
    A dismal thing to do!"
"The night is fine," the Walrus said,
    "Do you admire the view?

"It was so kind of you to come!
    And you are very nice!"
The Carpenter said nothing but
    "Cut us another slice.
I wish you were not quite so deaf—
    I've had to ask you twice!"

"It seems a shame," the Walrus said,
    "To play them such a trick,
After we've brought them out so far,
    And made them trot so quick!"
The Carpenter said nothing but
    "The butter's spread too thick!"

"I weep for you," the Walrus said:
    "I deeply sympathize."
With sobs and tears he sorted out
    Those of the largest size,
Holding his pocket-handkerchief
    Before his streaming eyes.

"O Oysters," said the Carpenter,
    "You've had a pleasant run!
Shall we be trotting home again?"
    But answer came there none—
And this was scarcely odd, because
    They'd eaten every one.

—*Lewis Carroll*

The Moron

See the happy moron,
He doesn't give a damn!
I wish I were a moron—
My God! Perhaps I am!

—*Anonymous*

Marriage Couplet

I think of my wife, and I think of Lot,
And I think of the lucky break he got.

—*William Cole*

The Pobble Who Has No Toes

The Pobble who has no toes
   Had once as many as we;
When they said, "Some day you may lose
    them all";—
   He replied,—"Fish Fiddle dee-dee!"
And his Aunt Jobiska made him drink,
Lavender water tinged with pink,
For she said, "The World in general knows
There's nothing so good for a Pobble's toes!"

The Pobble who has no toes,
   Swam across the Bristol Channel;
But before he set out he wrapped his nose
   In a piece of scarlet flannel.
For his Aunt Jobiska said, "No harm
Can come to his toes if his nose is warm;
And it's perfectly known that a Pobble's toes
Are safe,—provided he minds his nose."

The Pobble swam fast and well
  And when boats or ships came near him
He tinkledy-binkledy-winkled a bell
  So that all the world could hear him.
And all the Sailors and Admirals cried,
When they saw him nearing the further
    side,—
"He has gone to fish, for his Aunt Jobiska's
Runcible Cat with crimson whiskers!"

But before he touched the shore,
  The shore of Bristol Channel,
A sea-green Porpoise carried away
  His wrapper of scarlet flannel.
And when he came to observe his feet
Formerly garnished with toes so neat
His face at once became forlorn
On perceiving that all his toes were gone!

And nobody ever knew
    From that dark day to the present,
Who so had taken the Pobble's toes,
    In a manner so far from pleasant.
Whether the shrimps or crawfish gray,
Or crafty Mermaids stole them away—
Nobody knew; and nobody knows
How the Pobble was robbed of his twice five
        toes!

The Pobble who has no toes
    Was placed in a friendly Bark,
And they rowed him back, and carried him up,
    To his Aunt Jobiska's Park.
And she made him a feast of his earnest wish
Of eggs and buttercups fried with fish;—
And she said,—"It's a fact the whole world
        knows,
That Pobbles are happier without their toes."

—*Edward Lear*

How Doth the Little Crocodile

How doth the little crocodile
    Improve his shining tail;
And pour the waters of the Nile
    On every golden scale!

How cheerfully he seems to grin,
    How neatly spreads his claws,
And welcomes little fishes in,
    With gently smiling jaws!

—*Lewis Carroll*

The Smoking World

Tobacco is a dirty weed:
  I like it.
It satisfies no normal need:
  I like it.
It makes you thin, it makes you lean,
It takes the hair right off your bean,
It's the worst darn stuff I've ever seen:
  I like it.

—*Graham Lee Hemminger*

Nightmare

When you're lying awake with a dismal
  headache, and repose is taboo'd by
  anxiety,
I conceive you may use any language you
  choose to indulge in, without
  impropriety;
For your brain is on fire—the bedclothes
  conspire of usual slumber to plunder
  you:
First your counterpane goes, and uncovers
  your toes, and your sheet slips
  demurely from under you;
Then the blanketing tickles—you feel like
  mixed pickles so terribly sharp is the
  pricking,
And you're hot, and you're cross, and you
  tumble and toss till there's nothing
  'twist you and the ticking.

Then the bedclothes all creep to the ground
   in a heap, and you pick 'em all up in a
   tangle;
Next your pillow resigns and politely
   declines to remain at its usual
   angle!
Well, you get some repose in the form of a
   doze, with hot eyeballs and head ever
   aching,
But your slumbering teems with such
   horrible dreams that you'd very much
   better be waking;
For you dream you are crossing the Channel,
   and tossing about in a steamer from
   Harwich—
Which is something between a large bathing
   machine and a very small second-class
   carriage—

And you're giving a treat (penny ice and cold
   meat) to a party of friends and
   relations—
They're a ravenous horde—and they all came
   on board at Sloane Square and South
   Kensington Stations.
And bound on that journey you find your
   attorney (who started that morning from
   Devon);
He's a bit undersized, and you don't feel
   surprised when he tells you he's only
   eleven.
Well, you're driving like mad with this
   singular lad (by-the-by the ship's now
   a four wheeler),
And you're playing round games, and he calls
   you bad names when you tell him that
   'ties pay the dealer';

But this you can't stand, so you throw up your
hand, and you find you're as cold as an icicle,
In your shirt and your socks (the black silk
with gold clocks), crossing Salisbury
Plain on a bicycle:
And he and the crew are on bicycles too—
which they've somehow or other
invested in—
And he's telling the tars, all the particulars of
a company he's interested in—
It's a scheme of devices, to get at low prices,
all goods from cough mixtures to cables
(Which tickled the sailors) by treating
retailers, as though they were all
vegetables—
You get a good spadesman to plant a small
tradesman, (first take off his booth with
a boot-tree),

And his legs will take root, and his fingers
   will shoot, and they'll blossom and bud
   like a fruit-tree—
From the greengrocer tree you get grapes and
   green pea, cauliflower, pineapple, and
   cranberries,
While the pastrycook plant, cherry brandy
   will grant, apple puffs, and three-
   corners, and banberries—
The shares are a penny, and ever so many are
   taken by Rothschild and Baring,
And just as a few are allotted to you, you
   awake with a shudder despairing—
You're a regular wreck, with a crick in you
   neck, and no wonder you snore, for
   your head's on the floor, and you've
   needles and pins from your soles to
   your shins, and your flesh is a-creep for

your left leg's asleep, and you've cramp
in your toes, and a fly on your nose,
and some fluff in your lung, and a
feverish tongue, and a thirst that's
intense, and a general sense that you
haven't been sleeping in clover;
But the darkness has passed, and it's daylight
at last, and the night has been long—
ditto ditto my song—and thank
goodness they're both of them over!

—*W. S. Gilbert*

Limericks

I'd rather have fingers than toes,
I'd rather have ears than a nose;
   As for my hair,
    I'm glad it's still there,
I'll be awfully sad when it goes.

—*Gelett Burgess*

*   *   *

There was a young lady of Ryde,
Who ate some green apples and died;
   The apples fermented
   Inside the lamented,
And made cider inside her inside.

—*Anonymous*

* * *

A man hired by John Smith and Co.
Loudly declared that he'd tho.
   Men that he saw
   Dumping dirt near his door—
The drivers, therefore, didn't do.

—*Mark Twain*

* * *

There was an old man of Tarentum,
Who gnashed his false teeth till he bent 'em:
   And when asked for the cost
   Of what he had lost,
Said, "I really can't tell, for I rent 'em!"

There were three young women of
   Birmingham,
And I know a sad story concerning 'em:
   They stuck needles and pins
   In the reverend shins
Of the Bishop engaged in confirming 'em.

There was a young lady of Wilts,
Who walked up to Scotland on stilts;
   When they said it was shocking
   To show so much stocking,
She answered: "Then what about kilts?"

   There was a young girl of Lahore,
   The same shape behind as before.
     As you never knew where
     To offer a chair,
   She had to sit down on the floor.

—*Cosmo Monkhouse*

My Own Epitaph

Life is a jest, and all things show it;
I thought so once, but now I know it.

—*John Gay*

The Height of the Ridiculous

I wrote some lines once on a time
  In a wondrous merry mood,
And though, as usual, men would say
  They were exceeding good.

They were so queer, so very queer,
  I laughed as I would die;
Albeit in the general way,
  A sober man am I.

I called my servant, and he came;
  How kind it was of him,
To mind a slender man like me,
  He of the mighty limb!

"These to the printer," I exclaimed,
  And, in my humorous way,
I added (as a trifling jest),
  "There'll be the devil to pay."

He took the paper, and I watched,
   And saw him peep within;
At the first line he read, his face
   Was all upon a grin.

He read the next, the grin grew broad,
   And shot from ear to ear;
He read the third, a chuckling noise
   I now began to hear.

The fourth, he broke into a roar;
   The fifth, his waistband split;
The sixth, he burst five buttons off,
   And tumbled in a fit.

Ten days and nights, with sleepless eye,
   I watched that wretched man,
And since, I never dare to write
   As funny as I can.

—*Oliver Wendell Holmes*

The Owl and the Pussy-Cat

The Owl and the Pussy-cat went to sea
   In a beautiful pea-green boat,
They took some honey, and plenty of money
   Wrapped up in a five-pound note.
The Owl looked up to the stars above,
   And sang to a small guitar,
"O lovely Pussy! O Pussy, my love,
   What a beautiful Pussy you are,
     You are,
     You are!
   What a beautiful Pussy you are!"

Pussy said to the Owl, "You elegant fowl!
   How charmingly sweet you sing!
O let us be married! too long we have tarried:
   But what shall we do for a ring?"
They sailed away, for a year and a day,
   To the land where the Bong-tree grows

And there in a wood a Piggy-wig stood
   With a ring at the end of his nose,
     His nose,
     His nose,
   With a ring at the end of his nose.

"Dear Pig, are you willing to sell for one
     shilling
   Your ring?" Said the Piggy, "I will."
So they took it away, and were married next
     day
   By the Turkey who lives on the hill.
They dined on mince, and slices of quince,
   Which they ate with a runcible spoon;
And hand in hand, on the edge of the sand,
   They dance by the light of the moon,
     The moon,
     The moon,
   They danced by the light of the moon.

—*Edward Lear*

Father William

"You are old, Father William" the young
    man said,
  "And your hair has become very white;
And yet you incessantly stand on your head—
  Do you think, at your age, it is right?"

"In my youth," Father William replied to his
    son,
  "I feared it might injure the brain;
But now that I'm perfectly sure I have none,
  Why, I do it again and again."

"You are old," said the youth, "as I
    mentioned before,
  And have grown most uncommonly fat;
Yet you turned a back somersault in at the
    door—
  Pray, what is the reason for that?"

"In my youth," said the sage, as he shook his
　　gray locks,
　"I kept all my limbs very supple
By the use of this ointment—one shilling the
　　box—
　Allow me to sell you a couple."

"You are old," said the youth, "and your jaws
　　are too weak
　For anything tougher than suet;
Yet you finished the goose, with the bones
　　and the beak;
　Pray, how did you manage to do it?"

"In my youth," said his father, "I took to the
　　law,
　And argued each case with my wife;
And the muscular strength which it gave to
　　my jaw,
　Has lasted the rest of my life."

"You are old," said the youth; "one would
      hardly suppose
   That your eye was as steady as ever;
Yet you balanced an eel on the end of your
      nose—
   What made you so awfully clever?"

"I have answered three questions, and that is
      enough,"
   Said his father, "don't give yourself airs!
Do you think I can listen all day to such stuff?
   Be off, or I'll kick you down-stairs!"

—*Lewis Carroll*

How Pleasant to
Know Mr. Lear

How pleasant to know Mr. Lear!
   Who has written such volumes of stuff!
Some think him ill-tempered and queer,
   But a few think him pleasant enough.

His mind is concrete and fastidious,
   His nose is remarkably big;
His visage is more or less hideous,
   His beard it resembles a wig.

He has ears, and two eyes, and ten fingers,
   Leastways if you reckon two thumbs;
Long ago he was one of the singers,
   But now he is one of the dumbs.

He sits in a beautiful parlor,
   With hundreds of books on the wall;
He drinks a great deal of Marsala,
   But never gets tipsy at all.

He has many friends, laymen and clerical,
    Old Foss is the name of his cat;
His body is perfectly spherical,
    He weareth a runcible hat.

When he walks in a waterproof white,
    The children run after him so!
Calling out, "He's come out in his night-
    gown, that crazy old Englishman, oh!"

He weeps by the side of the ocean,
    He weeps on the top of the hill;
He purchases pancakes and lotion,
    And chocolate shrimps from the mill.

He reads, but he cannot speak, Spanish,
    He cannot abide ginger beer:
Ere the days of his pilgrimage vanish,
    How pleasant to know Mr. Lear!

—*Edward Lear*

The Purple Cow

I never saw a Purple Cow,
I never hope to see one;
But I can tell you, anyhow,
  I'd rather see than be one.

—*Gelett Burgess*

To Minerva

My temples throb, my pulses boil,
  I'm sick of Song and Ode, and Ballad—
So, Thyrsis, take the Midnight Oil
  And pour it on a lobster salad.

—*Thomas Hood*

An Elegy on That Glory of Her Sex, Mrs. Mary Blaize

Good people all, with one accord,
    Lament for Madame Blaize,
Who never wanted a good word—
    From those who spoke her praise.

The needy seldom pass'd her door,
    And always found her kind;
She freely lent to all the poor,—
    Who left a pledge behind.

She strove the neighbourhood to please,
    With manners wond'rous winning,
And never followed wicked ways,—
    Unless when she was sinning.

At church, in silks and satins new,
    With hoops of monstrous size,
She never slumber'd in her pew,—
    But when she shut her eyes.

Her love was sought, I do aver,
　By twenty beaux and more;
The king himself has followed her,—
　When she has walk'd before.

But now her wealth and finery fled,
　Her hangers-on cut short all;
The doctors found, when she was dead,—
　Her last disorder mortal.

Let us lament, in sorrow sore,
　For Kent-street well may say,
That had she lived a twelve-month more,—
　She had not died today.

—*Oliver Goldsmith*

Madame Dill

Madame Dill
Is very ill,
And nothing will improve her,
Until she sees
The Tuileries
And waddles through the Louvre.

—*Anonymous*

Dinner in a Quick Lunch Room

Soup should be heralded with a mellow horn,
Blowing clear notes of gold against the stars;
Strange entrees with a jangle of glass bars
Fantastically alive with subtle scorn;
Fish, by a plopping, gurgling rush of waters,
Clear, vibrant waters, beautifully austere;
Roast, with a thunder of drums to stun the ear,
A screaming fife, a voice from ancient slaughters!

Over the salad let the woodwinds moan;
Then the green silence of many watercresses;
Dessert, a balalaika, strummed alone;
Coffee, a slow, low singing no passion stresses;
Such are my thoughts as—clang! crash! bang!—I
   brood
And gorge the sticky mess these fools call food!

—*Stephen Vincent Benet*

Harlem Hopscotch

One foot down, then hop! It's hot.
   Good things for the ones that's got.
Another jump, now to the left.
   Everybody for hisself.

In the air, now both feet down.
   Since you black, don't stick around.
Food is gone, the rent is due,
   Curse and cry and then jump two.

All the people out of work,
   Hold for three, then twist and jerk.
Cross the line, they count you out.
   That's what hopping's all about.

Both feet flat, the game is done.
They think I lost. I think I won.

—*Maya Angelou*

"I'm Nobody! Who Are You?"

I'm nobody! Who are you?
Are you—Nobody—too?
Then there's a pair of us?
Don't tell! They'd advertise—you know!

How dreary—to be—Somebody!
How public—like a Frog—
To tell one's name—the livelong June—
To an admiring Bog!

—Emily Dickinson

In Extremis

I saw my toes the other day.
I han't looked at them for months.
Indeed they might have passed away.
And yet they were my best friends once.
When I was small I knew them well.
I counted on them up to ten
And put them in my mouth to tell
The larger from the lesser. Then
I loved them better than my ears,
My elbows, adenoids, and heart.
But with the swelling of the years
We drifted, toes and I, apart.
Now, gnarled and pale, each said, *j'accuse!*—
I hid them quickly in my shoes.

—*John Updike*

One Art

The art of losing isn't hard to master;
so many things seem filled with the intent
to be lost that their loss is no disaster.

Lose something every day. Accept the fluster
of lost door keys, the hour badly spent.
The art of losing isn't hard to master.

Then practice losing farther, losing faster:
places, and names, and where it was you meant
to travel. None of these will bring disaster.

I lost my mother's watch. And look! my last, or
next-to-last, of three loved houses went.
The art of losing isn't hard to master.

I lost two cities, lovely ones. And, vaster,
some realms I owned, two rivers, a continent.
I miss them, but it wasn't a disaster.

—Even losing you (the joking voice, a gesture
I love) I shan't have lied. It's evident
the art of losing's not too hard to master
though it may look like (*Write* it!) like disaster.

—*Elizabeth Bishop*

AMERICANA ⌒

The Shooting of Dan McGrew

A bunch of the boys were whooping it up in
   The Malamute saloon;
The kid that handles the music-box was
   hitting a jag-time tune;
Back of the bar, in a solo game, sat Dangerous
   Dan McGrew,
And watching his luck, was his light-o'-love,
   the lady that's known as Lou.

When out of the night, which was fifty below,
   and into the din and the glare,
There stumbled a miner fresh from the
   creeks, dog-dirty, and loaded for bear.
He looked like a man with a foot in the grave
   and scarcely the strength of a louse,
Yet he tilted a poke of dust on the bar, and he
   called for drinks for the house.
There was none could place the stranger's face,
   though we searched ourselves for a clue;

But we drank his health, and the last to drink
   was Dangerous Dan McGrew.

There's men that somehow just grip your
   eyes, and hold them hard like a spell;
And such was he, and he looked to me like a
   man who had lived in hell;
With a face most fair, and the dreary stare of
   a dog whose day is done,
As he watered the green stuff in his glass, and
   the drops fell one by one.
Then I got to figgering who he was, and
   wondering what he'd do,
And I turned my head— and there watching
   him was the lady that's known as Lou.

His eyes went rubbering round the room, and
   he seemed in a kind of daze,

Till at last that old piano fell in the way of his
wandering gaze.
The rag-time kid was having a drink; there
was no one else on the stool,
So the stranger stumbles across the room, and
flops down there like a fool.
In a buckskin shirt that was glazed with dirt
he sat, and I saw him sway;
Then he clutched the keys with his talon
hands—my God! but that man could
play.

Were you ever out in the Great Alone, when
the moon was awful clear,
And the icy mountains hemmed you in with a
silence you most could hear;
With only the howl of a timber wolf, and you
camped there in the cold,

A half-dead thing in a stark, dead world,
    clean mad for the muck called gold;
While high overhead, green, yellow and red,
    the North Lights swept in bars?—
Then you've a hunch what the music meant
    . . . hunger and night and the stars.

And hunger not of the belly kind, that's
    banished with bacon and beans,
But the gnawing hunger of lonely men for a
    home and all that it means;
For a fireside far from the cares that are, four
    walls and a roof above;
But oh! so cramful of cozy joy, and crowned
    with a woman's love—
A woman dearer than all the world, and true
    as Heaven is true—
(God! how ghastly she looks through her
    rouge,—the lady that's known as Lou.)

Then on a sudden the music changed, so soft
    that you scarce could hear;
But you felt that your life had been looted
    clean of all that it once held dear;
That someone had stolen the woman you
    loved; that her love was a devil's lie;
That your guts were gone, and the best for
    you was to crawl away and die.
'Twas the crowning cry of a heart's
    despair, and it thrilled you through and
    through—
"I guess I'll make it a spread misere," said
    Dangerous Dan McGrew.

The music almost died away . . . then it burst
    like a pent-up flood;
And it seemed to say, "Repay, repay," and
    my eyes were blind with blood.

The thought came back of an ancient wrong,
     and it stung like a frozen lash,
And the lust awoke to kill, to kill . . . then the
     music stopped with a crash,
And the stranger turned, and his eyes they
     burned in a most peculiar way;
In a buckskin shirt that was glazed with dirt
     he sat, and I saw him sway;
Then his lips went in in a kind of grin, and he
     spoke, and his voice was calm,
And "Boys," says he, "you don't know me,
     and none of you care a damn;
"But I want to state, and my words are straight,
     and I'll bet my poke they're true,
"That one of you is a hound of hell . . . and that
     one is Dan McGrew."

Then I ducked my head, and the lights went
  out, and two guns blazed in the dark,
And a woman screamed, and the lights went
  up, and two men lay stiff and stark.
Pitched on his head, and pumped full of lead,
  was Dangerous Dan McGrew,
While the man from the creeks lay clutched
  to the breast of the lady that's known as Lou.

These are the simple facts of the case, and I
  guess I ought to know.
They say that the stranger was crazed with
  "hooch," and I'm not denying it's so.
I'm not so wise as the lawyer guys, but
  strictly between us two—
The woman that kissed him and—pinched
  his poke—was the lady that's known as
  Lou.

—*Robert W. Service*

Yankee Doodle

Yankee Doodle went to town
    Riding on a pony,
Stuck a feather in his cap
    And called it "macaroni."

Chorus:
Yankee Doodle, keep it up,
Yankee Doodle, dandy,
Mind the music and the step,
And with the girls be handy.

Father and I went down to camp,
    Along with Captain Gooding,
And there we see the men and boys,
    As thick as hasty pudding.

And there we see a thousand men,
    As rich as 'Squire David;
And what they wasted every day,
    I wish it could be saved.

The 'lasses they eat every day,
    Would keep a house in winter,
They have so much that, I'll be bound,
    They eat it when they're a mind to.

And there we see a swamping gun,
    Large as a log of maple,
Upon a deuced little cart,
    A load for father's cattle.

And every time they shot it off,
    It takes a horn of powder,
And makes a noise like father's gun,
    Only a nation louder.

—*Anonymous*

America

My country, 'tis of thee,
Sweet land of liberty,
  Of thee I sing;
Land where my father died,
Land of the pilgrims' pride,
From every mountain-side
  Let freedom ring.

My native country, thee,
Land of the noble free,
  Thy name I love;
I love thy rocks and rills,
Thy woods and templed hills;
My heart with rapture thrills,
  Like that above.

Let music swell the breeze,
And ring from all the trees
   Sweet freedom's song;
Let mortal tongues awake,
Let all that breathe partake,
Let rocks their silence break.—
   The sound prolong.

Our father's God, to Thee,
Author of liberty,
   To Thee we sing;
Long may our land be bright
With freedom's holy light;
Protect us by Thy might,
   Great God, our King.

—*Samuel Francis Smith*

America the Beautiful

O beautiful for spacious skies,
   For amber waves of grain,
For purple mountain majesties
   Above the fruited plain!
America! America!
   God shed His grace on thee
And crown thy good with brotherhood
   From sea to shining sea!

O beautiful for pilgrim feet,
   Whose stern, impassioned stress
A thoroughfare for freedom beat
   Across the wilderness!
America! America!
   God mend thine every flaw,
Confirm thy soul in self-control,
   Thy liberty in law!

O beautiful for heroes proved
   In liberating strife,
Who more than self their country loved,
   And mercy more than life!
America! America!
   My God thy gold refine,
Till all success be nobleness
   And every gain divine!

O beautiful for patriot dream
   That sees beyond the years
Thine alabaster cities gleam
   Undimmed by human tears!
America! America!
   God shed His grace on thee
And crown thy good with brotherhood
   From sea to shining sea!

—*Katharine Lee Bates*

The Star-Spangled Banner

O, say, can you see, by the dawn's early
  light,
   What so proudly we hailed at the twilight's
    last gleaming,
Whose broad stripes and bright stars though
    the perilous fight,
  O'er the ramparts we watched were so
    gallantly streaming?
And the rockets' red glare, the bombs
    bursting in air,
Gave proof thro' the night that our flag was
   still there.
O, say, does that star-spangled banner yet
    wave
O'er the land of the free, and the home of the
    brave!

On the shore, dimly seen thro' the mists of
    the deep,
  Where the foe's haughty host in dread
    silence reposes,
What is that which the breeze o'er the
    towering steep,
  As it fitfully blows, half conceals, half
    discloses?
Now it catches the gleam of the morning's
    first beam,
In full glory reflected, now shines on the
    stream.
'Tis the star-spangled banner; oh, long may it
    wave
O'er the land of the free, and the home of the
    brave!

And where is that band who so vauntingly
    swore
  That the havoc of war and the battle's
    confusion
A home and a country should leave us no
    more?
  Their blood was washed out their foul
    footsteps' pollution.
No refuge could save the hireling and slave
From the terror of flight, or the gloom of the
    grave:
And the star-spangled banner in triumph doth
    wave
O'er the land of the free, and the home of the
    brave!

Oh, thus be it ever when freemen shall stand
　　Between their loved homes and the war's
　　　desolation;
Blest with victory and peace, may the
　　　heaven-rescued land
　　Praise the power that hath made and
　　　preserved us a nation!
Then conquer we must, when our cause it is
　　　just,
And this be out motto: "In God is our trust!"
And the star-spangled banner in triumph doth
　　　wave,
O'er the land of the free, and the home of the
　　　brave!

—*Francis Scott Key*

Tribute to America

There is a people mighty in its youth,
  A land beyond the oceans of the west,
Where, though with rudest rites, Freedom
    and Truth
  Are Worshipt. From a glorious mother's
    breast,
  Who, since high Athens fell, among the rest
Sate like the Queen of Nations, but in woe,
  By inbred monsters outraged and opprest,
Turns to her chainless child for succor now,
It draws the milk of power in Wisdom's
    fullest flow.

That land is like an eagle, whose young gaze
  Feeds on the noontide beam, whose golden
    plume
Floats moveless on the storm, and on the blaze
  Of sunrise gleams when Earth is wrapt in
    gloom;
  An epitaph of glory for thy tomb

Of murdered Europe may thy fame be made,
Great People! As the sands shalt thou become,
Thy growth is swift as morn when night must
    fade;
The multitudinous Earth shall sleep beneath
    thy shade.

Yes, in the desert, is built a home
  For Freedom! Genius is made strong to rear
The monuments of man beneath the dome
  Of a new Heaven; myriads assemble there
  Whom the proud lords of man, in rage or
    fear,
Drive from their wasted homes. The boon I
    pray
  Is this—that Cythna shall be convoyed
    there,—
Nay, start not at the name—America!

—*Percy Bysshe Shelley*

Oh! Susanna

I come from Alabama,
Wid my banjo on my knee,
I'm g'wan to Louisiana,
My true love for to see.
It rain'd all night the day I left,
The weather it was dry;
The sun so hot I froze to death;
Susanna, don't you cry.

Chorus:
Oh! Susanna,
Don't you cry for me,
I come from Alabama
Wid my banjo on my knee.

I jumped aboard de telegraph,
And trabbeled down de ribber,
De lectric fluid magnified,
And killed five hundred nigger;

De bullgine bust, de horse run off,
I really thought I'd die;
I shut my eyes to hold my breath:
Susanna, don't you cry.

I had a dream de udder night,
When eb'ryting was still;
I thought I saw Susanna,
A coming down de hill;
De buckwheat-cake was in her
  mouth,
De tear was in her eye;
Says I, I'm coming from de South
Susanna, don't you cry.

I soon will be in New Orleans,
And den I'll look all round,
And when I find Susanna,
I'll fall upon the ground.
But if I do not find her,
Dis darkey'l surely die;
And when I'm dead and buried,
Susanna, don't you cry.

Stephen Foster

Dixie

I wish I was in de land ob cotton,
Old time dar am not forgotten;
   Look away, look away, look away,
    Dixie land!
In Dixie land whar I was born in,
Early on one frosty mornin',
   Look away, look away, look away,
    Dixie land!

Chorus:
Den I wish I was in Dixie! Hooray! Hooray!
In Dixie's land we'll take our stand, to lib an'
   die in Dixie,
Away, away, away down south in Dixie!
Away, away, away down south in Dixie!

Old missus marry Will de weaber,
William was a gay deceaber.
When he put his arm around 'er,
Looked as fierce as a forty-pounder.
His face was sharp as a butcher cleaber,
But dat did not seem to greab 'er;
Will run away, missus took a decline, O,
Her face was the color of bacon rhine, O.

While missus libbed, she libbed in clover,
When she died, she died all over;
How could she act de foolish part,
An' marry a man to break her heart?

Buckwheat cakes an' stony batter
Makes you fat or a little fatter;
Here's a health to de next old missus,
An' all de gals dat want to kiss us.

Now if you want to drive 'way sorrow,
Come an' hear dis song to-morrow;
Den hoe it down an' scratch your grabble,
To Dixie's land I'm bound to trabble.

—*Daniel Decatur Emmett*

The Cowboy's Lament

As I walked out on the streets of Laredo,
As I walked out in Laredo one day,
I spied a poor cowboy wrapped up in white
   linen,
Wrapped up in white linen as cold as the
   clay.

"Oh, beat the drum slowly and play the fife
   lowly,
Play the dead march as you carry me along;
Take me to the green valley, there lay the sod
   o'er me,
For I'm a young cowboy and I know I've
   done wrong.

"I see by your outfit that you are a cowboy"—
These words he did say as I boldly stepped
   by.

"Come sit down beside me and hear my sad
    story;
I am shot in the breast and I know I must die.

"Let sixteen gamblers come handle my coffin,
Let sixteen cowboys come sing me a song.
Take me to the graveyard and lay the sod o'er
    me,
For I'm a poor cowboy and I know I've done
    wrong.

"My friends and relations they live in the
    Nation,
They know not where their boy has gone.
He first came to Texas and hired to a
    ranchman,
Oh, I'm a young cowboy and I know I've
    done wrong.

"It was once in the saddle I used to go
    dashing;
It was once in the saddle I used to go gay;
First to the dram-house and then to the card-
    house;
Got shot in the breast and I am dying today.

"Get six jolly cowboys to carry my coffin;
Get six pretty maidens to bear up my pall.
Put bunches of roses all over my coffin,
Put roses to deaden the sods as they fall.
"Then swing your rope slowly and rattle your
    spurs lowly,
And give a wild whoop as you carry me along;
And in the grave throw me and roll the sod
    o'er me
For I'm young cowboy and I know I've
    done wrong.

"Oh, bury beside me my knife and six-
   shooter,
My spurs on my heel, my rifle by my side,
And over my coffin put a bottle of brandy
That the cowboys may drink as they carry me
   along.

"Go bring me a cup, a cup of cold water,
To cool my parched lips," the cowboy then
   said;
Before I returned his soul had departed,
And gone to the round-up—the cowboy was
   dead.

We beat the drum slowly and played the fife
   lowly,
And bitterly wept as we bore him along;

For we all loved our comrade, so brave,
   young, and handsome,
We all loved our comrade although he'd done
   wrong.

Where men lived raw, in the desert's maw,
And hell was nothing to shun;
Where they buried 'em neat, without
   preacher or sheet,
And writ on their foreheads, crude but
   sweet,
"This Jasper was slow with a gun."

—*Anonymous*

The Big Rock Candy Mountains

One evening as the sun went down
And the jungle fire was burning,
Down the track came a hobo hiking.
And he said, "Boys, I'm not turning,
I'm headed for a land that's far away,
Beside the crystal fountains,
So come with me, we'll go and see
The Big Rock Candy Mountains."

In the Big Rock Candy Mountains,
There's a land that's fair and bright,
Where the handouts grow on bushes,
And you sleep out every night.
Where the boxcars all are empty,
And the sun shines every day
On the birds and the bees,
And the cigarette trees,
And the lemonade springs
Where the Bluebird sings
In the Big Rock Candy Mountains.

In the Big Rock Candy Mountains
All the cops have wooden legs,
And the bulldogs all have rubber teeth,
And the hens lay softboiled eggs.
There the farmer's trees are full of fruit,
And the barns are full of hay,
And I'm bound to go
Where there ain't no snow,
And the rain don't fall,
And the wind don't blow
In the Big Rock Candy Mountains.

In the Big Rock Candy Mountains
You never change your socks,
And the little streams of alcohol
Come a-trickling down the rocks.
There ain't no shorthandled shovels,
No axes, spades, or picks,
And I'm bound to stay
Where they sleep all day,
Where they hung the Turk

That invented work
In the Big Rock Candy Mountains.

In the Big Rock Candy Mountains
All the jails are made of tin,
And you can walk right out again
As soon as you are in.
Where the brakemen have to tip their hats,
And the railroad bulls are blind,
There's a lake of stew,
And a gin lake, too,
You can paddle all around 'em
In a big canoe
In the Big Rock Candy Mountains.

—*Anonymous*

Casey at the Bat

The outlook wasn't brilliant for the Mudville
   nine that day;
The score stood four to two with but one
   inning more to play.
And then, when Cooney died at first, and
   Barrows did the same,
A sickly silence fell upon the patrons of the
   game.

A straggling few got up to go in deep despair.
   The rest
Clung to that hope which springs eternal in
   the human breast;
They thought, If only Casey could but get a
   whack at that
We'd put up even money now, with Casey at
   the bat.

But Flynn preceded Casey, as did also Jimmy
   Blake,
And the former was a lulu and the latter was a
   cake;
So upon that stricken multitude grim
   melancholy sat,
For there seemed but little chance of Casey's
   getting to the bat.

But Flynn let drive a single, to the
   wonderment of all,
And Blake, the much despisèd, tore the cover
   off the ball;
And when the dust had lifted, and men saw
   what had occurred,
There was Jimmy safe at second, and Flynn
   a-hugging third.

Then from five thousand throats and more
  there rose a lusty yell;
It rumbled through the valley, it rattled in the
  dell;
It knocked upon the mountain and recoiled
  upon the flat,
For Casey, mighty Casey, was advancing to
  the bat.

There was ease in Casey's manner as he
  stepped into his place;
There was pride in Casey's bearing and a
  smile on Casey's face.
And when, responding to the cheers, he
  lightly doffed his hat,
No stranger in the crowd could doubt 'twas
  Casey at the bat.

Ten thousand eyes were on him as he rubbed
  his hands with dirt,
Five thousand tongues applauded when he
  wiped them on his shirt;
Then while the writhing pitcher ground the
  ball into his hip,
Defiance gleamed from Casey's eye, a sneer
  curled Casey's lip.

And now the leather-covered sphere came
  hurtling through the air,
And Casey stood a-watching it in haughty
  grandeur there.
Close by the sturdy batsman the ball
  unheeded sped;
"That ain't my style," said Casey. "Strike
  one," the umpire said.

From the benches, black with people, there
    went up a muffled roar,
Like the beating of the storm waves on a
    stern and distant shore.
"Kill him! Kill the umpire!" shouted someone
    on the stand;
And it's likely they'd have killed him had not
    Casey raised his hand.

With a smile of Christian charity great
    Casey's visage shone;
He stilled the rising tumult, he bade the
    game go on;
He signaled to the pitcher, and once more the
    spheroid flew;
But Casey still ignored it, and the umpire
    said, "Strike two."

"Fraud!" cried the maddened thousands, and
    echo answered "Fraud!"
But one scornful look from Casey and the
    audience was awed;
They saw his face grow stern and cold, they
    saw his muscles strain,
And they knew that Casey wouldn't let that
    ball go by again.

The sneer is gone from Casey's lip, his teeth
    are clenched in hate,
He pounds with cruel violence his bat upon
    the plate;
And now the pitcher holds the ball, and now
    he lets it go,
And now the air is shattered by the force of
    Casey's blow.

Oh, somewhere in this favored land the sun is
   shining bright,
The band is playing somewhere, and
   somewhere hearts are light;
And somewhere men are laughing, and
   somewhere children shout,
But there is no joy in Mudville—mighty
   Casey has struck out.

—*Ernest Lawrence Thayer*

Bill Bailey, Won't You Please Come Home?

On one summer's day,
Sun was shining fine,
De lady love of old Bill Bailey
Was hanging clothes on de line
In her back yard
And weeping hard;
She married a B. and O. brakeman,
Dat took and throw'd her down.
Bellering like a prune-fed calf,
Wid a big gang hanging 'round;
And to dat crowd,
She yelled out loud:

"Won't you come home, Bill Bailey, won't
  you come home?"
She moaned de whole day long.
"I'll do de cooking, darling, I'll pay de rent;
I knows I've done you wrong.

'Member dat rainy eve dat I drove you out
Wid nothing but a fine tooth comb!
I know I'se to blame, well ain't dat a shame?
Bill Bailey, won't you please come home?"

Bill drove by dat door
In an automobile,
A great big diamond, coach and footman,
Hear dat big wench squeal:
"He's all alone,"
I heard her groan;
She hollered thro' dat door:
"Bill Bailey, is you sore?
Stop a minute won't you listen to me?
Won't I see you no more?"
Bill winked his eye,
As he heard her cry: *(Repeat refrain)*

—Hughie Cannon

A Poem on Table Manners, Used by a Shaker Community in 1868

We found of these bounties
   Which heaven does give,
That some live to eat,
   And that some eat to live—
That some think of nothing
   But pleasing the taste,
And care very little
   How much they do waste.

Tho' heaven has bless'd us
   With plenty of food;
Bread, butter, and honey,
   And all that is good;
We loathe to see mixtures
   Where gentle folk dine,
Which scarcely look fit
   For the poultry or swine.

We often find left,
  On the same china dish,
Meat, apple-sauce, pickle,
  Brown bread and minced fish;
Another's replenish'd
  With butter and cheese;
With pie, cake and toast,
  Perhaps added to these.

—*Anonymous*

Waltz Me Around Again, Willie

Willie Fitzgibbons who used to sell ribbons,
And stood up all day on his feet,
Grew very spooney on Madeline Mooney,
Who'd rather be dancing than eat.
Each evening she'd tag him, to some dance
    hall drag him,
And when the band started to play,
She'd up like a silly and grab tired Willie,
Steer him on the floor and she'd say:

Chorus:
"Waltz me around again, Willie, a-round,
    a-round, a-round,
The music it's dreamy, it's peaches and
    creamy,
Oh! don't let my feet touch the ground.

I feel like a ship on an ocean of joy,
I just want to holler out loud, 'Ship ahoy!'
Oh, waltz me around again, Willie, a-round,
  a-round, a-round,"

Willie De Vere was a dry goods cashier,
At his desk he would sit all the day,
Till his doctor advised him to start exercising,
Or else he would soon fade away.
One night this poor looney met Madeline
  Mooney,
Fitzgibbons then shouted with joy,
"She's a good health regainer, you've got a
  great trainer,
Just wait till she hollers, my boy. *(Repeat*
  chorus.)

—*Will D. Cobb*

Take Me Out to the Ball Game

Take me out to the ball game,
Take me out with the crowd.
Buy me some peanuts and Cracker Jack
I don't care if I never get back.
Let me root, root, root, for the home town,
If they don't win it's a shame,
For it's one, two, three strikes you're out
At the old ball game.

—*Jack Norworth*

Lizzie Borden

Lizzie Borden took an axe
And gave her mother forty whacks;
When she saw what she had done
She gave her father forty-one!

—*Anonymous*

Jesse James

It was on Wednesday night, the moon was
    shining bright,
  They robbed the Danville train.
And the people they did say, for many miles
    away,
'Twas the outlaws Frank and Jesse James.

Chorus:
Jesse had a wife to mourn him all her life,
  The children they are brave.
'Twas a dirty little coward shot Mister
    Howard,
  And laid Jesse James in his grave.

Jesse was a man was a friend to the poor,
  He never left a friend in pain.
And with his brother Frank he robbed the
    Chicago bank
  And then held up the Glendale train.

It was Robert Ford, the dirty little coward,
   I wonder how he does feel,
For he ate of Jesse's bread and he slept in
      Jesse's bed
   Then he laid Jesse James in his grave.

It was his brother Frank that robbed the
      Gallatin bank,
   And carried the money from the town.
It was in this very place that they had a little
      race,
   For they shot Captain Sheets to the ground.

They went to the crossing not very far from
      there,
   And there they did the same;
And the agent on his knees he delivered up
      the keys
To the outlaws Frank and Jesse James.

It was on a Saturday night, Jesse was at home
    Talking to his family brave,
When the thief and the coward, little Robert
        Ford,
    Laid Jesse James in his grave.

How people held their breath when they
        heard of Jesse's death,
    And wondered how he ever came to die.
'Twas one of the gang, dirty Robert Ford,
    That shot Jesse James on the sly.

Jesse went to rest with his hand on his breast;
    He died with a smile on his face.
He was born one day in the county of Clay,
    And came from a solitary race.

—*Anonymous*

From Pocahontas

Wearied arm, and broken sword
Wage in vain the desperate fight;
Round him press a countless horde,
He is but a single knight.
Hark! a cry of triumph shrill
Through the wilderness resounds,
As, with twenty bleeding wounds,
Sinks the warrior, fighting still.

Now they heap the funeral pyre,
And the torch of death they light;
Ah! 'tis hard to die by fire!
Who will shield the captive knight?
Round the stake with fiendish cry
Wheel and dance the savage crowd,
Cold the victim's mien and proud,
And his breast is bared to die.

Who will shield the fearless heart?
Who avert the murderous blade?
From the throng with sudden start
See, there springs an Indian maid.
Quick she stands before the knight:
"Loose the chain, unbind the ring!
I am daughter of the king,
And I claim the Indian right!"

Dauntlessly aside she flings
Lifted axe and thirsty knife,
Fondly to his heart she clings,
And her bosom guards his life!
In the woods of Powhatan
Still 'tis told by Indian fires
How a daughter of their sires
Saved a captive Englishman.

—*William Makepeace Thackeray*

Abraham Lincoln

(April 26, 1865)

Oh, slow to smite and swift to spare,
   Gentle and merciful and just!
Who, in the fear of God, didst bear
   The sword of power, a nation's trust!

In sorrow by the bier we stand,
   Amid the awe that hushes all,
And speak the anguish of a land
   That shook with horror at thy fall.

Thy task is done; the bond are free:
   We bear thee to an honored grave,
Whose proudest monument shall be
   The broken fetters of the salve.

Pure was thy life; its bloody close
   Hath placed thee with the sons of light,
Among the noble host of those
   Who perished in the cause of Right.

—*William Cullen Bryant*

Washington

Soldier and statesman, rarest unison;
High-poised example of great duties done
Simply as breathing, a world's honors worn
As life's indifferent gifts to all men born;
Dumb for himself, unless it were to God,
But for his barefoot soldier eloquent,
Tramping the snow to coral where they trod,
Held by his awe in hollow-eyed content;
Modest, yet firm as Nature's self; unblamed
Save by the men his nobler temper shamed;
Not honored then or now because he wooed
The popular voice, but that he still withstood;
Broad-minded, higher-souled, there is but
   one
Who was all this and ours and all men's—
   Washington.

—*James Russell Lowell*

Lucinda Matlock

From Spoon River Anthology

I went to the dances at Chandlerville,
And played snap-out at Winchester.
One time we changed partners,
Driving home in the moonlight of middle June,
And then I found Davis.
We were married and lived together for seventy
    years,
Enjoying, working, raising the twelve children,
Eight of whom we lost
Ere I had reached the age of sixty.
I spun, I wove, I kept the house, I nursed the sick,
I made the garden, and for holiday
Rambled over the fields where sang the larks,
And by Spoon River gathering many a shell,
And many a flower and medicinal weed—
Shouting to the wooded hills, singing to the
    green valleys.

At ninety-six I had lived enough, that is all,
And passed to a sweet repose.
What is this I hear of sorrow and weariness,
Anger, discontent and drooping hopes?
Degenerate sons and daughters,
Life is too strong for you—
It takes life to love Life.

—*Edgar Lee Masters*

Professor Newcomer

From Spoon River Anthology

Everyone laughed at Col. Prichard
For buying an engine so powerful
That it wrecked itself, and wrecked the grinder
He ran it with.
But here is a joke of cosmic size:
The urge of nature that made a man
Evolve from his brain a spiritual life—
Oh miracle of the world!—
The very same brain with which the ape and
    wolf
Get food and shelter and procreate themselves.
Nature has made man do this,
In a world where she gives him nothing to do
After all—(though the strength of his soul goes
    round
In a futile waste of power.
To gear itself to the mills of the gods)—
But get food and shelter and procreate himself!

—*Edgar Lee Masters*

I Hear America Singing

I hear America singing, the varied carols I hear,
Those of mechanics, each one singing his as it
    should be blithe and strong,
The carpenter singing his as he measures his
    plank or beam,
The mason singing his as he makes ready for
    work, or leaves off work,
The boatman singing what belongs to him in
    his boat, the deckhand singing on the
    steamboat deck,
The shoemaker singing as he sits on his bench,
    the hatter singing as he stands,
The wood-cutter's song, the ploughboy's on his
    way in the morning, or at noon
    intermission or at sundown,
The delicious singing of the mother, or of the
    young wife at work, or of the girl sewing
    or washing,

Each singing what belongs to him or her and
    to none else,
The day what belongs to the day—at night the
    party of young fellows, robust, friendly,
Singing with open mouths their strong
    melodious songs.

—*Walt Whitman*

The New Colossus

NOT like the brazen giant of Greek fame,
With conquering limbs astride from land to land;
Here at our sea-washed, sunset gates shall stand
A mighty woman with a torch, whose flame
Is the imprisoned lightning, and her name
Mother of Exiles. From her beacon-hand
Glows world-wide welcome; her mild eyes command
The air-bridged harbor that twin cities frame.
"Keep, ancient lands, your storied pomp!" cries she
With silent lips. "Give me your tired, your poor,
Your huddled masses yearning to breathe free,
The wretched refuse of your teeming shore.
Send these, the homeless, tempest-tost to me,
I lift my lamp beside the golden door!"

—*Emma Lazarus*

TRAVEL AND WORK

Sir Patrick Spence

The king sits in Dumferling toune,
Drinking the blude-reid wine:
"O whar will I get guid sailor,
   To sail this schip of mine?"

Up and spak and eldern knight,
   Sat at the kings richt kne:
"Sir Patrick Spence is the best sailor
   That sails upon the se."

The king has written a braid letter,
   And signed it wi his hand,
And sent it to Sir Patrick Spence,
   Was walking on the sand.

The first line that Sir Patrick red,
   Aloud lauch lauched he:
The next line that Sir Patrick red,
   The teir blinded his e'e.

"O what is this has don this deid,
  This ill deid don to me,
To send me out this time o' the yeir
  To sail upon the se!

"Mak hast, mak hast, my mirry men all,
  Our guid schip sails the morne:"
"O say na sae, my master deir,
  For I feir a deadlie storme.

"Late late yestreen I saw the new moone,
  Wi' the auld moone in hir arme,
And I feir, I feir, my deir master.
  That we will cum to harme."

O our Scots nobles wer richt laith
  To weer their cork-heild schoone;
Bot lang owre a' the play wer playd,
  Thair hats they swam aboone.

O lang, lang may their ladies sit,
  Wi' thair fans into their hand,
Or eir they se Sir Patrick Spence
  Cum sailing to the land.

O lang, lang may be the ladies stand,
Wi thair gold kems in their hair,
Waiting for thair ain deir lords,
  For they'll se thame na mair.

Haf owre, haf owre to Aberdour,
  It's fiftie fadom deip,
And thair lies guid Sir Patrick Spence,
  Wi' the Scots lords at his feit.

—*Anonymous*

The Wreck of the Hesperus

It was the Schooner Hesperus,
   That sailed the wintry sea;
And the skipper had taken his little daughter,
   To bear him company.

Blue were her eyes as the fairy-flax,
   Her cheeks like the dawn of day,
And her bosom white as the hawthorn buds,
   That ope in the month of May.

The skipper he stood beside the helm,
   His pipe was in his mouth,
And he watched how the veering flaw did blow
   The smoke now West, now South.

Then up and spake an old Sailòr,
   Had sailed to the Spanish Main,
"I pray thee, put into yonder port,
   For I fear a hurricane.

"Last night, the moon had a golden ring,
   And to-night no moon we see!"
The skipper, he blew a whiff from his pipe,
   And a scornful laugh laughed he.

Colder and Louder blew the wind,
   A gale form the Northeast,
The snow fell hissing in the brine,
   And the billows frothed like yeast.

Down came the storm, and smote amain
   The vessel in its strength;
She shuddered and paused, like a frightened
   steed,
   Then leaped her cable's length.

"Come hither! come hither! my little daughter,
   And do not tremble so;
For I can weather the roughest gale
   That ever wind did blow."

He wrapped her warm in his seaman's coat
    Against the stinging blast;
He cut a rope from a broken spar,
    And bound her to the mast.

"O father! I hear the church-bell ring,
    Oh say, what may it be?"
"'Tis a fog-bell on a rock-bound coast!"—
    And he steered for the open sea.

"O father! I hear the sound of guns,
    Oh say, what may it be?"
"Some ship in distress, that cannot live
    In such an angry sea!"

"O father! I see a gleaming light,
    Oh say, what may it be?"
But the father answered never a word,
    A frozen corpse was he.

Lashed to the help, all stiff and stark,
    With his face turned to the skies,
The lantern gleamed through the gleaming
    snow
    On his fixed and glassy eyes.

Then the maiden clasped her hands and
    prayed
    That savèd she might be;
And she thought of Christ, who stilled the
    wave,
    On the Lake of Galilee.

And fast through the midnight dark and drear,
    Through the whistling sleet and snow,
Like a sheeted ghost, the vessel swept
    Tow'rds the reef of Norman's Woe.

And ever the fitful gusts between
  A sound came from the land;
It was the sound of trampling surf
  On the rocks and the hard sea-sand.

The breakers were right beneath her bows,
  She drifted a dreary wreck,
And a whooping billow swept the crew
  Like icicles from her deck.

She struck where the white and fleecy waves
  Looked soft as carded wool,
But the cruel rocks, they gored her side
  Like the horns of an angry bull.

Her rattling shrouds, all sheathed in ice,
  With the masts went by the board;
Like a vessel of glass, she stove and sank,
  Ho! ho! the breakers roared!

At daybreak, on the bleak sea-beach,
  A fisherman stood aghast,
To see the form of a maiden fair,
  Lashed close to a drifting mast.

The salt sea was frozen on her breast,
  The salt tears in her eyes,
And he saw her hair, like the brown seaweed,
  On the billows fall and rise.

Such was the wreck of the Hesperus,
  In the midnight and the snow!
Christ save us all from a death like this,
  On the reef of Norman's Woe!

—*Henry Wadsworth Longfellow*

Up at a Villa— Down in the City

(As Distinguished by an Italian
Person of Quality)

Had I but plenty of money, money enough
  and to spare,
The house for me, no doubt, were a house in
  the city-square;
Ah, such a life, such a life, as one leads at the
  window there!

Something to see, by Bacchus, something to
  hear, at least!
There, the whole day long, one's life is a
  perfect feast;
While up at a villa one lives, I maintain it, no
  more than a beast.

Well now, look at our villa! stuck like the
    horn of a bull
Just on a mountain-edge as bare as the
    creature's skull,
Save a mere shag of a bush with hardly a leaf
    to pull!
—I scratch my own, sometimes, to see if the
    hair's turned wool.

But the city, oh the city—the square with the
    houses! Why?
They are stone-faced, white as a curd, there's
    something to take the eye!
Houses in four straight lines, not a single
    front awry;
You watch who crosses and gossips, who
    saunters, who hurries by;
Green blinds, as a matter of course, to draw
    when the sun gets high;
And the shops with fanciful signs which are
    painted properly.

What of a villa? Though winter be over in
   March by rights,
'Tis May perhaps ere the snow shall have
   withered well off the heights:
You've the brown ploughed land before,
   where the oxen steam and wheeze,
And the hills over-smoked behind by the
   faint gray olive-trees.

Is it better in May, I ask you? You've summer
   all at once;
In a day he leaps complete with a few strong
   April suns.
'Mid the sharp short emerald wheat, scarce
   risen three fingers well,
The wild tulip, at the end of its tube, blows
   out its great red bell
Like a thin clear bubble of blood, for the
   children to pick and sell.

Is it ever hot in the square? There's a
    fountain to spout and splash!
In the shade it sings and springs: in the shine
    such foam-bows flash
On the horses with curling fish-fails, that
    prance and paddle and pash
Round the lady atop in her conch—fifty
    gazers do not abash,
Though all that she wears is some weeds
    round her waist in a sort of sash.

All the year long at the villa, nothing to see
    though you linger,
Except yon cypress that points like death's
    lean lifted fore-finger.
Some think fireflies pretty, when they mix i'
    the corn and mingle,
Or third the stinking hemp till the stalks of it
    seem a-tingle.

Late August or early September, the stunning
  cicala is shrill,
And the bees keep their tiresome whine
  round the resinous firs on the hill.
Enough of the seasons,—I spare you the
  months of the fever and chill.

Ere you open your eyes in the city, the
  blessed church-bells begin:
No sooner the bells leave off than the
  diligence rattles in:
You get the pick of the news, and it costs you
  never a pin.
By-and-by there's the traveling doctor gives
  pills, lets blood, draws teeth;
Or the Pulcinello-trumpet breaks up the
  market beneath.
At the post-office such a scene-picture—the
  new play, piping hot!

And a notice how only this morning, three
   liberal thieves were shot.
Above it, behold the Archbishop's most
   fatherly of rebukes,
And beneath, with his crown and his lion,
   some little new law of the Duke's !
Or a sonnet with flowery marge, to the
   Reverend Don So-and-so,
Who is Dante, Boccaccio, Petrarca, Saint
   Jerome, and Cicero,
"And moreover" (the sonnet goes rhyming),
   "the skirts of Saint Paul has reached,
Having preached us those six Lent-lectures
   more unctuous than ever he preached."
Noon strikes,—here sweeps the procession!
   our Lady borne smiling and smart
With a pink gauze gown all spangles, and
   seven swords stuck in her heart!

Bang-whang-whang goes the drum, *tootle-te-tootle* the fife;
No keeping one's haunches still: it's the
greatest pleasure in life.

But bless you, it's dear—it's dear! fowls,
wine, at double the rate.
They have clapped a new tax upon salt, and
what oil pays passing the gate
It's a horror to think of. And so, the villa for
me, not the city!
Beggars can scarcely be choosers: but still—
ah, the pity, the pity!
Look, two and two go the priests, then the
monks with cowls and sandals,
And the penitents dressed in white shirts,
a-holding the yellow candles;
One, he carries a flag up straight, and another
a cross with handles,

And the Duke's guard brings up the rear, for
the better prevention of scandals:
Bang-whang-whang goes the drum, *tootle-te-
tootle* the fife.
Oh, a day in the city-square, there is no such
pleasure in life!

—*Robert Browning*

Home-Thoughts from Abroad

Oh, to be in England
Now that April's there,
And whoever wakes in England
Sees, some morning, unaware,
That the lowest boughs and the brush-wood
   sheaf
Round the elm-tree bole are in tiny leaf,
While the chaffinch sings on the orchard bough
In England—now!

And after April, when May follows,
And the whitethroat builds, and all the
   swallows—
Hark! where my blossomed pear-tree in the
   hedge
Leans to the field and scatters on the clover
Blossoms and dewdrops—at the bent-spray's
   edge—

That's the wise thrush; he sings each song
   twice over,
Lest you should think he never could
   recapture
The first fine careless rapture!
And though the fields look rough with hoary
   dew,
All will be gay when noontide wakes anew
The buttercups, the little children's dower,
—Far brighter than this gaudy melon-flower!

—*Robert Browning*

The Village Blacksmith

Under a spreading chestnut-tree
   The village smithy stands;
The smith, a might man is he,
   With large and sinewy hands;
And the muscles of his brawny arms
   Are strong as iron bands.

His hair is crisp, and black, and long,
   His face is like the tan;
His brow is wet with honest sweat,
   He earns whate'er he can,
And looks the whole world in the face,
   For he owes not any man.

Week in, week out, from morn till night,
   You can hear his bellows blow;
You can hear him swing his heavy sledge
   With measured beat and slow,

Like a sexton ringing the village bell,
　　When the evening sun is low.

And children coming home from school
　　Look in at the open door;
They love to see the flaming forge,
　　And hear the bellows roar,
And catch the burning sparks that fly
　　Like chaff from a threshing-floor.

He goes on Sunday to the church,
　　And sits among his boys;
He hears the parson pray and preach,
　　He hears his daughter's voice,
Singing in the village choir,
　　And it makes his heart rejoice.

It sounds to him like her mother's voice,
　　Singing in Paradise!

He needs must think of her once more,
  How in the grave she lies;
And with his hard, rough hand he wipes
  A tear our of his eyes.

Toiling,—rejoicing,—sorrowing,
  Onward through life he goes;
Each morning sees some task begin,
  Each evening sees its close;
Something attempted, something done,
  Has earned a night's repose.

Thanks, thanks to thee, my worthy friend,
  For the lesson thou hast taught!
Thus at the flaming forge of life
  Our fortunes must be wrought;
Thus on its sounding anvil shaped
  Each burning deed and thought!

—*Henry Wadsworth Longfellow*

London

I wander through each chartered street,
Near where the chartered Thames does flow,
And mark in every face I meet,
Marks of weakness, marks of woe.

In every cry of every man,
In every infant's cry of fear,
In every voice, in every ban
The mind-forged manacles I hear.

How the chimney-sweeper's cry
Every blackening church appalls;
And the hapless soldier's sigh
Runs in blood down palace walls.

But most through midnight streets I hear
How the youthful harlot's curse
Blasts the new-born infant's tear,
And blights with plagues the marriage hearse.

—*William Blake*

Rome

Rome is but nature's twin, which has reflected
  Rome.
We see its civic might, the signs of its decorum
In the transparent air, the firmament's blue
  dome,
The colonnades of groves and in the meadow's
  forum.

—*Osip Emilevitch Mandelstam*

Chicago

Hog Butcher for the World,
Tool maker, Stacker of Wheat,
Player with Railroads and the Nation's
     Freight Handler;
Stormy, husky, brawling,
City of the Big Shoulders:

They tell me you are wicked and I believe
     them, for I have seen your painted
     women under the gas lamps luring the
     farm boys.
And they tell me you are crooked and I
     answer: Yes, it is true I have seen the
     gunman kill and go free to kill again.
And they tell me you are brutal and my reply
     is: On the faces of women and children
     I have seen the mark of wanton
     hunger.

And having answered so I turn once more to
   those who sneer at this my city, and I
   give them back the sneer and say to them:
Come and show me another city with lifted
   head singing so proud to be alive and
   coarse and strong and cunning.
Flinging magnetic curses amid the toil of
   piling job on job, here is a tall bold
   slugger set vivid against the little soft
   cities;
Fierce as a dog with tongue lapping for
   action, cunning as a savage pitted
   against the wilderness,
     Bareheaded,
     Shoveling,
     Wrecking,
     Planning,
     Building, breaking, rebuilding.

Under the smoke, dust all over his mouth,
    laughing with white teeth,
Under the terrible burden of destiny laughing
    as a young man laughs,
Laughing even as an ignorant fighter laughs
    who has never lost a battle,
Bragging and laughing that under his wrist is
    the pulse,
And under his ribs the heart of the people,
        Laughing!
Laughing the stormy, husky, brawling
    laughter of Youth, half-naked,
    sweating, proud to be Hog Butcher,
    Tool Maker, Stacker of Wheat, Player
    with Railroads and Freight Handler to
    the Nation.

—*Carl Sandburg*

My City

When I come down to sleep death's endless
   night,
The threshold of the unknown dark to cross,
What to me then will be the keenest loss,
When this bright world blurs on my fading
   sight?
Will it be that no more I shall see the trees
Or smell the flowers or hear the singing birds
Or watch the flashing streams or patient herds?
No, I am sure it will be none of these.

But, ah! Manhattan's sights and sounds, her
   smells,
Her crowds, her throbbing force, the thrill
   that comes
From being of her a part, her subtile spells,
Her shining towers, her avenues, her slums—
O God! the stark, unutterable pity,
To be dead, and never again behold my city!

—*James Weldon Johnson*

The Tired Worker

O whisper, I my soul! The afternoon
Is waning into evening, whisper soft!
Peace, O my rebel heart! for soon the moon
From out its misty veil will swing aloft!
Be patient, weary body, soon the night
Will wrap thee gently in her sable sheet,
And with a leaden sigh thou wilt invite
To rest thy tired hands and aching feet.
The wretched day was theirs, the night is
    mine;
Come, tender sleep, and fold me to thy breast.
But what steals out the gray clouds red like
    wine?
O dawn! O dreaded dawn! O let me rest!
Weary my veins, my brain, my life! Have pity!
No! Once again the harsh, the ugly city.

—*Claude McKay*

The Rime of the Ancient Mariner

Part I

It is an ancient mariner,
And he stoppeth one of three.
'By thy long grey beard and glittering eye,
Now wherefore stopp'st thou me?

The bridegroom's doors are opened wide,
And I am next of kin;
The guests are met, the feast is set:
May'st hear the merry din.'

He holds him with his skinny hand,
'There was a ship,' quoth he.
'Hold off! unhand me, grey-beard loon!'
Eftsoons his hand dropt he.

He holds him with his glittering eye—
The wedding-guest stood still,
And listens like a three years' child:
The Mariner hath his will.

The wedding-guest sat on a stone:
He cannot choose but hear;
And thus spake on that ancient man,
The bright-eyed mariner.

'The ship was cheered, the harbour cleared,
Merrily did we drop
Below the kirk, below the hill,
Below the lighthouse top.

The sun came up upon the left,
Out of the sea came he!
And he shone bright, and on the right
Went down into the sea.

Higher and higher every day,
Till over the mast at noon—'
The wedding-guest here beat his breast,
For he heard the loud bassoon.

The bride hath paced into the hall,
Red as a rose is she;
Nodding their heads before her goes
The merry minstrelsy.

The wedding-guest he beat his breast,
Yet he cannot choose but hear;
And thus spake on that ancient man,
The bright-eyed mariner.

And now the storm-blast came, and he
Was tyrannous and strong:
He struck with his o'ertaking wings,
And chased us south along.

With sloping masts and dipping prow,
As who pursued with yell and blow
Still treads the shadow of his foe,
And forward bends his head,
The ship drove fast, loud roared the blast,
And southward aye we fled.

And now there came both mist and snow,
And it grew wondrous cold:
And ice, mast-high, came floating by,
As green as emerald.

And through the drifts the snowy clifts
Did send a dismal sheen:
Nor shapes of men nor beasts we ken—
The ice was all between.

The ice was here, the ice was there,
The ice was all around:
It cracked and growled, and roared and howled,
Like noises in a swound!

At length did cross an albatross,
Thorough the fog it came;
As if it had been a Christian soul,
We hailed it in God's name.

It ate the food it ne'er had eat,
And round and round it flew.
The ice did split with a thunder-fit;
The helmsman steered us through!

And a good south wind sprung up behind;
The albatross did follow,
And every day, for food or play,
Came to the mariner's hollo!

In mist or cloud, on mast or shroud,
It perched for vespers nine;
Whiles all the night, through fog-smoke white,
Glimmered the white Moon-shine.'

'God save thee, ancient mariner!
From the fiends, that plague thee thus!—
Why look'st thou so?'—With my cross-bow
I shot the albatross.

—*Samuel Taylor Coleridge*

The Helmsman

O Be swift—
we have always known you wanted us.

We fled inland with our flocks,
we pastured them in hollows,
cut off from the wind
and the salt track of the marsh.

We worshipped inland—
we stepped past wood-flowers,
we forgot your tang,
we brushed wood-grass.
We wandered from pine-hills
through oak and scrub-oak tangles,
we broke hyssop and bramble,
we caught flower and new bramble-fruit
in our hair: we laughed
as each branch whipped back,
we tore our feet in half buried rocks
and knotted roots and acorn-cups.

We forgot—we worshipped,
we parted green from green,
we sought further thickets,
we dipped our ankles
through leaf-mould and earth,
and wood and wood-bank enchanted us—

and the feel of the clefts in the bark,
and the slope between tree and tree—
and a slender path strung field to field

and wood to wood
and hill to hill
and the forest after it.

We forgot—for a moment
tree-resin, tree-bark,
sweat of a torn branch
were sweet to the taste.

We were enchanted with the fields,
the tufts of coarse grass
in the shorter grass—
we loved all this.

But now, our boat climbs—hesitates—drops—
climbs—hesitates—crawls back—
climbs—hesitates—
O be swift—
we have always known you wanted us.

—H.D. *(Hilda Doolittle)*

On the Road to Nowhere

On the road to nowhere
What wild oats did you sow
When you left your father's house
With your cheeks aglow?
Eyes so strained and eager
To see what you might see?
Were you thief or were you fool
Or most nobly free?

Were the tramp-days knightly,
True sowing of wild seed?
Did you dare to make the songs
Vanquished workmen need?
Did you waste much money
To deck a leper's feast?
Love the truth, defy the crowd
Scandalize the priest?
On the road to nowhere
What wild oats did you sow?

Stupids find the nowhere-road
Dusty, grim and slow.

Ere their sowing's ended
They turn them on their track,
Look at the caitiff craven wights
Repentant, hurrying back!
Grown ashamed of nowhere,
Of rags endured for years,
Lust for velvet in their hearts,
Pierced with Mammon's spears,
All but a few fanatics
Give up their darling goal,
Seek to be as others are,
Stultify the soul.
Reapings now confront them,
Glut them, or destroy,
Curious seeds, grain or weeds
Sown with awful joy.

Hurried is their harvest,
They make soft peace with men.
Pilgrims pass. They care not,
Will not tramp again.

O nowhere, golden nowhere!
Sages and fools go on
To your chaotic ocean,
To your tremendous dawn.
Far in your fair dream-haven,
Is nothing or is all...
They press on, singing, sowing
Wild deeds without recall!

—*Vachel Lindsay*

In the Train

Fields beneath a quilt of snow
From which the rocks and stubble sleep,
And in the west a shy white star
That shivers as it wakes from deep.
The restless rumble of the train,
The drowsy people in the car,
Steel blue twilight in the world,
And in my heart a timid star.

— *Sara Teasdale*

Aunt Jemima's Quilt

A MIRACLE of gleaming dyes,
　　Blue, scarlet, buff and green;
O ne'er before by mortal eyes
　　Such gorgeous hues were seen!
So grandly was its plan designed,
　　So cunningly 'twas built,
The whole proclaimed a master mind—
　　My Aunt Jemima's quilt.

Each friendly household far and wide
　　Contributed its share;
It chronicled the country side
　　In colors quaint and rare.
From belles and brides came rich brocade
　　Enwrought with threads of gilt;
E'en buxom widows lent their aid
　　To Aunt Jemima's quilt.

No tapestry from days of yore,
  No web from Orient loom,
But paled in beauteous tints before
  This strange expanse of bloom.
Here glittering stars and comets shone
  O'er flowers that never wilt;
Here fluttered birds from worlds unknown
  On Aunt Jemima's quilt.

O, merry was the quilting bee,
  When this great quilt was done;
The rafters rang with maiden glee,
  And hearts were lost and won.
Ne'er did a throng of braver men
  In war dash hilt to hilt,
Than sought the smiles of beauty then
  Round Aunt Jemima's quilt.

This work of art my aunt esteemed
  The glory of the age;
No poet's eyes have ever beamed
  More proudly o'er his page.
Were other quilt to this compared,
  Her nose would upward tilt;
Such impudence was seldom dared
  O'er Aunt Jemima's quilt.

Her dear old hands have gone to dust,
  That once were lithe and light;
Her needles keen arc thick with rust,
  That flashed so nimbly bright.
And here it lies by her behest,
  Stained with the tears we spilt,
Safe folded in this cedar chest —
  My Aunt Jemima's quilt.

—*Samuel Minturn Peck*

The Voyage

Outward! Sail ever on thy mystic voyages,
Cut loose, up anchor from the shores of
   thought!
There leave in safety all the dull world's
   countless captives,
Seek thou the freedom only thou hast sought.

Thine are the prophets, thine the few, the poets,
   martyrs,
Stung with the impulse of divine surmise;
Thy chosen ventured while the millions feared
   and faltered,
Realized the rapture, dared the great surprise.

Outward! For, ever as of old, the deep sea's
   distance,
Ever new skies to lift and lighten, lie
Far down the dusk of day-break from the
   shores proved pathways
Pathless to perilous eternity.

Yea! tho' the friendly wharves are all aflame
  with faces,
Yea! tho' their anger rave in foolish sound,—
Outward!—Their hands would hinder but their
  hearts are fearful;
Leave them their fetters, Thou shalt not be
  bound!

What tho' they cry —"Time's hosts have trod
  our ways of life out,
Roads, charts and lamplight, —ours the valued
  prize,
The proved!" Thou sayest —"My goal how dim,
  my seas how trackless,
My risks how vast!" Then leave them to their lies!

Shake down the sails to catch the blood-red
  drift of sunset!
Haste! lest they hold thee slave among the slaves.

Thou shalt be outcast of their laws and scorned
and homeless:
The sin the world blames is the sin that saves.

Outward! The sail full-breasted swells against
the night-fall,
And now the world where blind men lead the
blind,
The world of laws and lies, of safety and
obedience,
The prize, the conflict, —all is left behind!

Outward! O haste! The flushed fresh mouth of
dawn is calling!
Outward! O space at last! O light at last!
Steer where the comrades wait thee, journeying
still, still outward,
Wise in a conscious and perfected past.

—*George Cabot Lodge*

The Arrival

The ship glides softly in,
Mist clings about the harbour;
The muddy, oily Hudson
Is scattered with driftwood darkening the tide;

The ship glides in and stops.
The tide has ebbed all night and now will turn.
Grey wraiths, the skyscrapers
Loom in the mist, white smoke about them
    blowing.

Dense, dreary rain
Lashes the waters of the harbour;
The air hangs flat, unstirring,
The land looms, dead ahead.

The dark, lead-coloured piers
Covered with roofs, crouch low beside the
    shore;
The ship glides near to one of these and turns.
Beyond the city lies, rain-veiled.

Tugs gliding easily,
Brown tugs with pilot-houses perched atop,
Windowed with glass, their poised gilt eagles
    shining,
Nose up between the swinging ship and the
    shore,

The Henry K. Jewett fastens to her bows.
The Brandon follows
Puffing soft-coal smoke in dense feathery
    billows;
The Martin B. Flannery finds a midship berth.

Tug after tug assembles,
One after the other till nine tugs are gathered.
A dense array of funnels, black, dun, red,
Between the waiting ship and the pier head.
Then on a sudden they release their steam.

With rocking shocks, with throb of beating
    engines,

With plumed salutes Of smoke above slim
  funnels,
With racing shake of blades that trample up
  the water,
They keep their blunt beaks pressed against our
  side.

Minute on minute passes:
The ship hangs yet unstirring.
Out of the pilot-houses faces peer
And stare up at the wallowing bulk beyond.

Nine columns of flying smoke
Blue-black or feathery-grey, upcurled and
  hurried,
Rise tumbling to the sky
In shadowy rushing hosts to bar our inward
  path,

And still the ship stirs not.
She fights the swirl of water by her side,
Till a tenth tug, from somewhere suddenly
   summoned,
Comes tooting up her whistle, loudly,
Out of the dense grey fog, half-filled with
   waving ferry boats.

Then, suddenly,
The sheer white bows swing inward,
Quivering in every fibre,
Towards the waiting dock-end of the shed.

One after one the tugs slip off,
Backing and churning at the raging water.
The weary ship slips in
'To the dark quiet of her berth at last;

So you, America,
Have taken men from their free-swinging gait

About the seas of the world, and pinned them
    to the shore,
By the harsh effort of your shoving hands.

—*John Gould Fletcher*

Passengers

At the gate, I sit in a row of blue seats
With the possible company of my death,
this sprawling miscellany of people—
carry-on bags and paperbacks—

That could be gathered in a flash
into a band of pilgrims on the last open road.
Not that I think
if our plane crumpled into a mountain ·

we would all ascend together,
holding hands like a ring of skydivers,
into a sudden gasp of brightness,
or that there would be some common place

for us to reunite to jubilize the moment,
some spaceless, pillarless Greece
where we could, at the count of three,
toss our ashes into the sunny air.

It's just that the way that man has his briefcase
so carefully arranged,
the way that girl is cooling her tea,
and the flow of the comb that woman

passes through her daughter's hair…
and when you consider the altitude,
the secret parts of the engines,
and all the hard water and the deep canyons
   below…

well, I just think it would be good if one of us
maybe stood up and said a few words,
or, so as not to involve the police,
at least quietly wrote something down.

—*Billy Collins*

What Work Is

We stand in the rain in a long line
waiting at Ford Highland Park. For work.
You know what work is—if you're
old enough to read this you know what
work is, although you may not do it.
Forget you. This is about waiting,
shifting from one foot to another.
Feeling the light rain falling like mist
into your hair, blurring your vision
until you think you see your own brother
ahead of you, maybe ten places.
You rub your glasses with your fingers,
and of course it's someone else's brother,
narrower across the shoulders than
yours but with the same sad slouch, the grin
that does not hide the stubbornness,
the sad refusal to give in to
rain, to the hours wasted waiting,
to the knowledge that somewhere ahead
a man is waiting who will say, "No,
we're not hiring today," for any
reason he wants. You love your brother,

now suddenly you can hardly stand
the love flooding you for your brother,
who's not beside you or behind or
ahead because he's home trying to
sleep off a miserable night shift
at Cadillac so he can get up
before noon to study his German.
Works eight hours a night so he can sing
Wagner, the opera you hate most,
the worst music ever invented.
How long has it been since you told him
you loved him, held his wide shoulders,
opened your eyes wide and said those words,
and maybe kissed his cheek? You've never
done something so simple, so obvious,
not because you're too young or too dumb,
not because you're jealous or even mean
or incapable of crying in
the presence of another man, no,
just because you don't know what work is.
—*Philip Levine*

Hay For the Horses

He had driven half the night
From far down San Joaquin
Through Mariposa, up the
Dangerous Mountain roads,
And pulled in at eight a.m.
With his big truckload of hay
   behind the barn.
With winch and ropes and hooks
We stacked the bales up clean
To splintery redwood rafters
High in the dark, flecks of alfalfa
Whirling through shingle-cracks of light,
Itch of haydust in the
sweaty shirt and shoes.
At lunchtime under Black oak
Out in the hot corral,
—The old mare nosing lunchpails,
Grasshoppers crackling in the weeds—

"I'm sixty-eight" he said,
"I first bucked hay when I was seventeen.
I thought, that day I started,
I sure would hate to do this all my life.
And dammit, that's just what
I've gone and done."

—*Gary Snyder*

Hotel Insomnia

I liked my little hole,
Its window facing a brick wall.
Next door there was a piano.
A few evenings a month
a crippled old man came to play
"My Blue Heaven."

Mostly, though, it was quiet.
Each room with its spider in heavy overcoat
Catching his fly with a web
Of cigarette smoke and revery.
So dark,
I could not see my face in the shaving mirror.

At 5 A.M. the sound of bare feet upstairs.
The "Gypsy" fortuneteller,
Whose storefront is on the corner,
Going to pee after a night of love.

Once, too, the sound of a child sobbing.
So near it was, I thought
For a moment, I was sobbing myself.

—*Charles Simic*

WAR

Barbara Frietchie

(September 13, 1862)

Up from the meadows rich with corn,
Clear in the cool September morn,

The clustered spires of Frederick stand
Green-walled by the hills of Maryland.

Round about them orchards sweep,
Apple and peach tree fruited deep,

Fair as the garden of the Lord
To the eyes of the famished rebel horde,

On what pleasant morn of the early fall
When Lee marched over the mountain-wall;

Over the mountains winding down,
Horse and foot, into Frederick town.

Forty flags with their silver stars,
Forty flags with their crimson bars,

Flapped in the morning wind: the sun
Of noon looked down, and saw not one.

Up rose old Barbara Frietchie then,
Bowed with her fourscore years and ten;

Bravest of all in Frederick town,
She took up the flag the men hauled down;

In her attic window the staff she set,
To show that one heart was loyal yet.

Up the street came the rebel tread,
Stonewall Jackson riding ahead.

Under his slouched hat left and right
He glanced; the old flag met his sight.

"Halt!"—the dust-brown ranks stood fast.
"Fire!"—out blazed the rifle-blast.

It shivered the window, pane and sash;
It rent the banner with seam and gash

Quick as it fell, from the broken staff
Dame Barbara snatched the silken scarf.

She leaned far out on the window-sill,
And shook it forth with a royal will.

"Shoot, if you must, this old gray head,
But spare your country's flag," she said.

A shade of sadness, a blush of shame,
Over the face of the leader came;

The nobler nature within him stirred
To life at that woman's deed and word;

"Who touches a hair of yon gray head
Dies like a dog! March on!" he said.

All day long through Frederick street
Sounded the tread of marching feet:

All day long that free flag tossed
Over the heads of the rebel host.

Even its torn folds rose and fell
On the loyal winds that loved it well;

And through the hill-gaps sunset light
Shone over it with a warm good-night.

Barbara Frietchie's work is o'er,
And the Rebel rides on his raids no more.

Honor to her! and let a tear
Fall, for her sake, on Stonewall's bier.

Over Barbara Frietchie's grave,
Flag of Freedom and Union, wave!

Peace and order and beauty draw
Round thy symbol of light and law:

And ever the stars above look down
On thy stars below in Frederick town!

—*John Greenleaf Whittier*

The Charge of the Light Brigade

Half a league, half a league,
  Half a league onward,
All in the valley of Death
  Rode the six hundred.
"Forward, the Light Brigade!
Charge for the guns," he said:
Into the valley of Death
  Rode the six hundred.
"Forward, the Light Brigade!"
Was there a man dismay'd?
Not tho' the soldier knew
  Someone had blunder'd:
Theirs not to make reply,
Theirs not to reason why,
Theirs but to do and die:
Into the valley of Death
  Rode the six hundred.

Cannon to right of them,
Cannon to left of them,

Cannon in front of them
  Volley'd and thunder'd;
Strom'd at with shot and shell,
Boldly they rode and well,
Into the jaws of Death,
Into the mouth of Hell
  Rode the six hundred.

Flash'd all their sabers bare,
Flash'd as they turn'd in air
Sabring the gunners there,
Charging an army, while
  All the world wonder'd:
Plung'd in the battery-smoke
Right thro' the line they broke;
Cossack and Russian
Reel'd from the saber-stroke
  Shatter'd and sunder'd.
Then they rode back, but not,
  Not the six hundred.

Cannon to right of them,
Cannon to left of them,
Cannon behind them
   Volley'd and thunder'd;
Strom'd at with shot and shell,
While horse and hero fell,
They that had fought so well
Came thro' the jaws of Death,
Back from the mouth of Hell,
All that was left of them
   Left of six hundred.

When can their glory fade?
O the wild charge they made!
   All the world wonder'd.
Honor the charge they made!
Honor the Light Brigade,
   Noble six hundred!

—*Alfred, Lord Tennyson*

Concord Hymn

(Sung at the completion of the Concord Monument,
April 19, 1836)

By the rude bridge that arched the flood,
  Their flag to April's breeze unfurled,
Here once the embattled farmers stood,
  And fired the shot heard round the world.

The foe long since in silence slept;
  Alike the conqueror silent sleeps;
And Time the ruined bridge has swept
  Down the dark stream which seaward
    creeps.

On this green bank, by this soft stream,
  We set to-day a votive stone;
That memory may their deed redeem,
  When, like our sires, our sons are gone.

Spirit, that made those heroes dare
    To die, and leave their children free,
Bid Time and Nature gently spare
    The shaft we raise to them and thee.

—*Ralph Waldo Emerson*

Paul Revere's Ride

Listen, my children, and you shall hear,
Of the midnight ride of Paul Revere,
On the eighteenth of April, in Seventy-five;
Hardly a man is now alive
Who remembers that famous day and year.

* * *

He said to his friend, "If the British march
By land or sea from the town tonight,
Hang a lantern aloft in the belfry arch
Of the North Church tower as a signal light,—
One, if by land, and two, if by sea;
And I on the opposite shore will be,
Ready to ride and spread the alarm
Through every Middlesex village and farm,
For the country folk to be up and to arm."

Then he said, "Good night!" and with
    muffled oar
Silently rowed to the Charlestown shore,
Just as the moon rose over the bay,
Where swinging wide at her moorings lay
The Somerset, British man-of-war;
A phantom ship, with each mast and spar
Across the moon like a prison bar,
And a huge black hulk, that was magnified
By it own reflection in the tide.

Meanwhile, his friend through alley and
    street
Wanders and watches, with eager ears,
Till in the silence around him he hears
The muster of men at the barrack door,
The sound of arms, and the tramp of feet,
And the measured tread of the grenadiers,
Marching down to their boats on the shore.

Then he climbed the tower of the Old North
   Church,
By the wooden stairs, with stealthy tread,
To the belfry-chamber overhead,
And startled the pigeons from their perch
On the somber rafters, that round him made
Masses and moving shapes of shade,—
By the trembling ladder, steep and tall,
To the highest window in the wall,
Where he paused to listed and look down
A moment on the roofs of the town
And the moonlight flowing over all.

Beneath, in the churchyard, lay the dead,
In their night-encampment on the hill,
Wrapped in silence so deep and still
That he could hear, like a sentinel's tread,
The watchful night-wind, as it went
Creeping along from tent to tent,
And seeming to whisper, "All is well!"

A moment only he feels the spell
Of the place and the hour, and the secret
 dread
Of the lonely belfry and the dead;
For suddenly all his thoughts are bent
On a shadowy something far away,
Where the river widens to meet the bay,—
A line of black that bends and floats
On the rising tide, like a bridge of boats.

Meanwhile, impatient to mount and ride,
Booted and spurred, with a heavy stride
On the opposite shore walked Paul Revere.
Now he patted his horse's side,
Now gazed at the landscape far and near,
Then, impetuous, stamped the earth,
And turned and tightened his saddle girth;
But mostly he watched with eager search
The belfry's tower of the Old North Church,
As it rose above the graves on the hill,

Lonely and spectral and somber and still.
And lo! as he looks, on the belfry height
A glimmer, and then a gleam of light!
He springs to the saddle, the bridle he turns,
But lingers and gazes, till full of his sight
A second lamp in the belfry burns!

A hurry of hoofs in a village street,
A shape in the moonlight, a bulk in the dark,
And beneath, from the pebbles, in passing, a
   spark
Struck out by a steed flying fearless and fleet;
That was all! And yet, through the gloom and
   the light,
The fate of a nation was riding that night;
And the spark struck out by that steed, in his
   flight,
Kindled the land into flame with its heat.
He has left the village and mounted the steep,

And beneath him, tranquil and broad and deep,
Is the Mystic, meeting the ocean tides;
And under the alders that skirt its edge,
Now soft on the sand, now loud on the ledge,
Is heard the tramp of his steed as he rides.

It was twelve by the village clock,
When he crossed the bridge into Medford
    town.
He heard the crowing of the cock,
And the barking of the farmer's dog,
And he felt the damp of the river fog,
That rises after the sun goes down.
It was one by the village clock,
When he galloped into Lexington.
He saw the gilded weathercock
Swim in the moonlight as he passed,
And the meeting-house windows, blank and
    bare,

Gaze at him with a spectral glare,
As if they already stood aghast
At the bloody work they would look upon.

It was two by the village clock,
When he came to the bridge in Concord
   town.
He heard the bleating of the flock,
And the twitter of birds among the trees,
And felt the breath of the morning breeze
Blowing over the meadows brown.
And one was safe and asleep in his bed
Who at the bridge would be first to fall,
Who that day would be lying dead,
Pierced by a British musket-ball.

You know the rest. In books you have read,
How the British Regulars fired and fled,—
How the farmers gave them ball for ball,
From behind each fence and farmyard wall,

Chasing the redcoats down the lane,
Then crossing the fields to emerge again
Under the trees at the turn of the road,
And only pausing to fire and load.
So though the night rode Paul Revere;
And so through the night went his cry of
   alarm
To every Middlesex village and farm,—
A cry of defiance, and not of fear,
A voice in the darkness, a knock at the door,
And a word that shall echo for evermore!
For, borne on the night-wind of the Past,
Through all our history, to the last,
In the hour of darkness and peril and need,
The people will waken and listen to hear
The hurrying hoof-beats of that steed,
And the midnight message of Paul Revere.

—*Henry Wadsworth Longfellow*

The Marines' Hymn

From the Halls of Montezuma to the shores of
   Tripoli,
We fight our country's battles in the air, on
   land and sea,
First to fight for right and freedom
And to keep our honor clean,
We are proud to claim the title
Of United States Marines.

Our flag's unfurled to ev'ry breeze
From dawn to setting sun
We have fought in ev'ry clime and place
Where we could take a gun
In the snow of far-off northern lands
And in sunny tropic scenes
You will find us always on the job
The United States Marines.

Here's health to you and to our corps
Which we are proud to serve
In many a strife we've fought for life
And never lost our nerve
If the Army and the Navy
Ever look on heaven's scenes
They will find the streets are guarded
By United States Marines.

—*Anonymous*

Battle Hymn of the Republic

Mine eyes have seen the glory of the coming
   of the Lord:
He is trampling out the vintage where the
   grapes of wrath are stored;
He hath loosed the fateful lightning of his
   terrible swift sword;
   His truth is marching on.

Chorus:
Glory! glory! Hallelujah!
Glory! glory! Hallelujah!
Glory! glory! Hallelujah!
   His truth is marching on!

I have seen him in the watch-fires of a
   hundred circling camps;
They have builded him an altar in the
   evening dews and damps;

I can read his righteous sentence by the dim
   and flaring lamps:
      His day is marching on.

I have read a fiery gospel, write in burnished
   rows of steel:
"As ye deal with my contemners, so with you
   my grace shall deal;
Let the Hero, born of woman, crush the
   serpent with his heel,
      Since God is marching on."

He has sounded forth the trumpet that shall
   never call retreat;
He is sifting out the hearts of men before his
   judgment-seat;
Oh, be swift, my soul, to answer him! be
   jubilant, my feet!
      Our God is marching on.

In the beauty of the lilies Christ was born
across the sea,
With a glory in his bosom that transfigures
you and me:
As he died to make men holy, let us die to
make men free,
While God is marching on.

—*Julia Ward Howe*

When Johnny Comes Marching Home

When Johnny comes marching home again,
Hurrah! Hurrah!
We'll give him a hearty welcome then,
Hurrah! Hurrah!
The men will cheer, and the boys will shout,
The ladies they will all turn out,
And we'll all feel gay
When Johnny comes marching home.

The old church bell will peal with joy,
Hurrah! Hurrah!
To welcome home our darling boy,
Hurrah! Hurrah!
The village lads and lassies say
With roses they will strew the way,
And we'll all feel gay
When Johnny comes marching home.

Get ready for the Jubilee,
Hurrah! Hurrah!
We'll give the hero three times three,
Hurrah! Hurrah!
The laurel wreath is ready now
To place upon his loyal brow
And we'll all feel gay
When Johnny comes marching home.

—*Patrick S. Gilmore*

Shiloh

A Requiem (April 1862)

Skimming lightly, wheeling still,
  The swallows fly low
Over the field in clouded days,
  The forest-field of Shiloh—
Over the field where April rain
Solaced the parched one stretched in pain
Through the pause of night
That followed the Sunday fight
  Around the church of Shiloh—
The church so lone, the log-built one,
That echoed to many a parting groan
    And natural prayer
  Of dying foemen mingled there—
Foemen at morn, but friends at eve—
  Fame or country least their care:
(What like a bullet can undeceive!)
  But now they lie low,
While over them the swallows skim,
  And all is hushed at Shiloh.

—*Herman Melville*

The Modern Major-General

I am the very model of a modern Major-
   General,
I've information vegetable, animal, and
   mineral;
I know the kings of England, and I quote the
   fights historical,
From Marathon to Waterloo, in order
   categorical;
I'm very well acquainted, too, with matters
   mathematical,
I understand equations, both the simple and
   quadratical;
About binomial theorem I'm teeming with a
   lot o' news,
With interesting facts about the square of the
   hypotenuse.
I'm very good at integral and differential
   calculus,

I know the scientific name of beings
   animalculous.
In short, in matters vegetable, animal, and
   mineral,
I am the very model of a modern Major-
   General.

I know our mythic history—King Arthur's and
   Sir Caradoc's.
I answer hard acrostics, I've a pretty taste for
   paradox;
I quote in elegiacs all the crimes of
   Heliogabalus,
In conics I can floor peculiarities parabolous.
I tell undoubted Raphaels from Gerard Dows
   and Zoffanies,
I know the croaking chorus from the "Frogs"
   of Aristophanes;
Then I can hum a fugue, of which I've heard
   the music's din afore,

And whistle all the airs from that confounded
  nonsense "Pinafore."
Then I can write a washing-bill in Babylonic
  cuneiform,
And tell you every detail of Caractacus's
  uniform.
In short, in matters vegetable, animal, and
  mineral,
I am the very model of a modern Major-
  General.

In fact, when I know what is meant by
  "mamelon" and "ravelin,"
When I can tell at sight a Chassepôt rifle from
  a javelin,
When such affairs as sorties and surprises I'm
  more wary at,
And when I know precisely what is meant by
  Commissariat,

When I have learnt what progress has been
   made in modern gunnery,
When I know more of tactics than a novice in
   a nunnery,
In short, when I've a smattering of
   elementary strategy,
You'll say a better Major-General has never
   sat a gee—
For my military knowledge, though I'm
   plucky and adventury,
Has only been brought down to the
   beginning of the century.
But still in learning vegetable, animal, and
   mineral,
I am the very model of a modern Major-
   General!

—*W. S. Gilbert*

Anthem for Doomed Youth

What passing-bells for these who die as
   cattle?
Only the monstrous anger of the guns.
Only the stuttering rifles' rapid rattle
Can patter out their hasty orisons.
No mockeries now for them; no prayer nor
   bells,
Nor any voice of mourning save the choirs—
The shrill, demented choirs of wailing shells;
And bugles calling for them from sad shires.

What candles may be held to speed them all?
Not in the hands of boys, but in their eyes
Shall shine the holy glimmers of good-byes.
The pallor of girls' brows shall be their pall;
Their flowers the tenderness of patient minds,
And each slow dusk a drawing-down of blinds.

—*Wilfred Owen*

The Dying Airman

A handsome young airman lay dying,
And as on the tarmac he lay,
To the mechanics who round him came sighing,
These last dying words he did say:

'Take the cylinders out of my kidneys,
Take the connecting-rod out of my brains,
Take the cam-shaft from out of my backbone,
And assemble the engine again.'

—*Anonymous*

Two Poems from the War

Oh, not the loss of the accomplished thing!
Not dumb farewells, nor long relinquishment
Of beauty had, and golden summer spent,
And savage glory of the fluttering
Torn banners of the rain, and frosty ring
Of moon-white winters, and the imminent
Long-lunging seas, and glowing students bent
To race on some smooth beach the gull's wing:

Not these, nor all we've been, nor all we've
   loved,
The pitiful familiar names, had moved
Our hearts to weep for them; but oh, the star
The future is! Eternity's too wan
To give again that undefeated, far,
All-possible irradiance of dawn.

Like moon-dark, like brown water you escape,
O laughing mouth, O sweet uplifted lips.
Within the peering brain old ghosts take shape;
You flame and wither as the white foam slips
Back from the broken wave: sometimes a start,
A gesture of the hands, a way you own
Of bending that smooth head above your heart,—
Then these are varied, then the dream is gone.

Oh, you are too much mine and flesh of me
To seal upon the brain, who in the blood
Are so intense a pulse, so swift a flood
Of beauty, such unceasing instancy.
Dear unimagined brow, unvisioned face,
All beauty has become your dwelling place.

—*Archibald MacLeish*

Dulce et Decorum Est

Bent double, like old beggars under sacks,
Knock-kneed, coughing like hags, we cursed
   through sludge,
Till on the haunting flares we turned our backs
And towards our distant rest began to trudge.
Men marched asleep. Many had lost their boots
But limped on, blood-shod. All went lame;
   all blind;
Drunk with fatigue; deaf even to the hoots
Of tired, outstripped Five-Nines that dropped
   behind.

Gas! Gas! Quick boys!—An ecstasy of
   fumbling,
Fitting the clumsy helmets just in time;
But someone still was yelling out and
   tumbling,
And flound'ring like a man in fire or lime…

Dim, through the misty panes and thick green
    light,
As under a green sea, I saw him drowning.
In all my dreams, before my helpless sight,
He plunges at me, guttering, choking, drowning.

If in some smothering dreams you too could
    pace
Behind the wagon that we flung him in,
And watch the white eyes writhing in his face,
His hanging face, like a devil's sick of sin;
If you could hear, at every jolt, the blood
Come gargling from the froth-corrupted lungs,
Obscene as cancer, bitter as the cud
Of vile, incurable sores on innocent tongues,—
My friend, you would not tell such high zest
To children ardent for some desperate glory,
The old Lie: Dulce et decorum est

Pro patria mori.
The honey-feast of the berries has stunned them;
  they believe in heaven.
One more look, and the berries and bushed end.
The only thing to come now is the sea.
From between two hills a sudden wind funnels
  at me,
Sapping the phantom laundry in my face.
These hills are too green and sweet to have
  tasted salt.
I follow the hills' northern face, and the face is
  orange rock
That looks out on nothing, nothing but a great
  space
Of white and pewter lights, and a din like
  silversmiths
Beating and beating at an intractable metal.

—*Wilfred Owen*

Base Details

If I were fierce, and bald, and short of breath
I'd live with scarlet Majors at the Base,
And speed glum heroes up the line to death.
You'd see me with my puffy petulant face,
Guzzling and gulping in the best hotel,
Reading the Roll of Honour. "Poor young chap,"
I'd say—"I used to know his father well;
Yes, we've lost heavily in this last scrap."
And when the war is done and youth stone
   dead,
I'd toddle safely home and die—in bed.

—*Siegfried Sassoon*

Dover Beach

The sea is calm to-night.
The tide is full, the moon lies fair
Upon the straits;—on the French coast the light
Gleams and is gone; the cliffs of England stand
Glimmering and vast, out in the tranquil bay.
Come to the window, sweet is the night air!
Only, from the long line of spray
Where the sea meets the moon-blanch'd land,

Listen! you hear the grating roar
Of pebbles which the waves draw back, and
    fling,
At their return, up the high strand,
Begin, and cease, and then again begin,
With tremulous cadence slow, and bring
The eternal note of sadness in.

Sophocles long ago
Heard it on the Aegean, and it brought
Into his mind the turbid ebb and flow
Of human misery; we
Find also in the sound a thought,
Hearing it by this distant northern sea.

The Sea of Faith
Was once, too, at the full, and round earth's
    shore
Lay like the folds of a bright girdle furl'd.
But now I only hear
Its melancholy, long, withdrawing roar,
Retreating, to the breath
Of the night-wind, down the vast edges drear
And naked shingles of the world.

Ah, love, let us be true
To one another! for the world, which seems
To lie before us like a land of dreams,
So various, so beautiful, so new,
Hath really neither joy, nor love, nor light,

Nor certitude, nor peace, nor help for pain;
And we are here as on a darkling plain
Swept with confused alarms of struggle and
   flight,
Where ignorant armies clash by night.

—*Mathew Arnold*

To Lucasta on Going to the War—for the Fourth Time

It doesn't matter what's the cause,
  What wrong they say we're righting,
A curse for treaties, bonds and laws,
  When we're to do the fighting!
And since we lads are proud and true,
  What else remains to do?
Lucasta, when to France your man
Returns his fourth time, hating war,
Yet laughs as calmly as he can
  And flings an oath, but says no more,
That is not courage, that's not fear—
Lucasta he's a Fusilier,
  And his pride sends him here.

Let statesmen bluster, bark and bray,
  And so decide who started
This bloody war, and who's to pay,
  But he must be stout-hearted,

Must sit and stake with quiet breath,
  Playing at cards with Death.
Don't plume yourself he fights for you;
It is no courage, love, or hate,
But let us do the things we do;
  It's pride that makes the heart be great;
It is not anger, no, nor fear—
Lucasta he's a Fusilier,
  And his pride keeps him here.

—*Robert Graves*

Masses

When the battle was over,
And the fighter was dead, a man came toward
    him
And said to him: 'Do not die; I love you so!'
But the corpse, it was sad! Went on dying.

And two came near, and told him again and
    again:
'Do not leave us! Courage! Return to life!'
But the corpse, it was sad! Went on dying.

Millions of persons stood around him,
All speaking the same thing: 'Stay here
    brother!'
But the corpse, it was sad! Went on dying.

Then all the men on the earth
Stood around him; the corpse looked at them
    sadly, deeply moved;
He sat up slowly,
Put his arms around the first man; started to
    walk…

—*Cesar Vallejo*
From the Spanish; from España, Aparta De Me Este
Caliz… *(Translated by Robert Bly)*

Antrim

No spot on earth where men have so fiercely for
   ages of time
Fought and survived and cancelled each other,
Pict and Gael and Dane, McQuillan,
   Clandonnel, O'Neill,
Savages, the Scot, the Norman, the English,
Here in the narrow passage and the pitiless
   north, perpetual
Betrayals, relentless resultless fighting.
A random fury of dirks in the dark; a struggle
   for survival
Of hungry blind cells of life in the womb.
But now the womb has grown old, her strength
   has gone forth;
a few red carts in a fog creak flax to the dubs,
And sheep in the high heather cry hungrily
   that life is hard;
a plaintive peace; shepherds and peasants.

We have felt the blades meet in the flesh in a
   hundred ambushes
And the groaning blood bubble in the throat;
In a hundred battles the heavy axes bite the
   deep bone,
The mountain suddenly stagger and be darkened.
Generation on generation we have seen the
   blood of boys
And heard the moaning of women massacred,
The passionate flesh and nerves have flamed
   like pitchpine and fallen
And lain in the earth softly dissolving.
I have lain and been humbled in all these
   graves, and mixed new flesh
with the old and filled the hollow of my mouth
With maggots and rotten dust and ages of
   repose, I lie here and plot
the agony of resurrection.

—*Robinson Jeffers*

Hard Drive

With my back to the wall
And a foot in the door
And my shoulder to the wheel
I would drive through Seskinore.

With an ear to the ground
And my neck on the block
I would tend to my wound
In Belleek and Bellanaleck.

With a toe in the water
And a nose for trouble
And an eye to the future
I would drive through Derryfubble

And Dunnamanagh and Ballynascreen,
Keeping that wound green.

—*Paul Muldoon*

PERMISSIONS ACKNOWLEDGMENTS

INDEX OF AUTHORS ~

INDEX OF TITLES

INDEX OF FIRST LINES ∼